ANCIENT WONDERINGS

ANCIENT
WONDERINGS

JOURNEYS INTO PREHISTORIC BRITAIN

JAMES CANTON

**WILLIAM
COLLINS**

William Collins
An imprint of HarperCollins*Publishers*
1 London Bridge Street
London SE1 9GF

WilliamCollinsBooks.com

First published in the United Kingdom by William Collins in 2017

22 21 20 19 18 17
11 10 9 8 7 6 5 4 3 2 1

ISBN 978-0-00-817520-7

Designed and typeset in Shango and Palatino by Tom Cabot/ketchup
Printed and bound in Great Britain by Clays Ltd, St Ives plc.

Cover image: one of the Callanish standing stones, Lewis, Outer Hebrides, Scotland.
All photography facing chapter openers by the author.

Maps on pages 3, 51, 85, 123, 161, 205, 247 & 281 from 'Ordnance Survey Maps – Six-inch
England and Wales, 1842–1952'

Excerpt on page 33 © Seamus Heaney, 1966, 'At a Potato Digging', *Death of a Naturalist*, Faber & Faber Ltd.
Lyrics from 'England' by PJ Harvey on pages 41–2 reproduced by kind permission of Hot Head Music Ltd.
    All rights reserved.
Excerpt on page 295 © Aubrey Burl, 1994, *Prehistoric Stone Circles* (3rd edn), Shire Publications, used by
    permission of Bloomsbury Publishing Plc.
Excerpt on pages 80–1 © Margaret Elphinstone, 2009. Reprinted by permission of Canongate Books Ltd.

MIX
Paper from
responsible sources
FSC
www.fsc.org   **FSC® C007454**

FSC™ is a non-profit international organisation established to promote the responsible management of the
world's forests. Products carrying the FSC label are independently certified to assure consumers that they
come from forests that are managed to meet the social, economic and ecological needs of present and future
generations, and other controlled sources. Find out more about HarperCollins and the environment at
www.harpercollins.co.uk/green

TO MY MOTHER

CONTENTS

Wondering *noun*

rare an object of wonder, a marvel: OE

Oxford English Dictionary

PREFACE

This book was born from a certain obsessive desire to understand the ancient world. I set out to venture across Britain seeking those prehistoric sites and phenomena that most intrigued me. Many of those travels were sentimental journeys, imaginative voyages. Inevitably, my interest in ancient Britain widened to encompass a need to know and to understand something of the ancient mindsets that created ways of living on these isles, ritual practices in these landscapes. And as I did so, my wonder took me ever deeper into time past.

I became a student of the ancient world. I learnt to step more carefully through the simplistic divisions between Stone, Bronze and Iron Ages. I learnt to recognise the magic of technological revolutions, such as that of metalworking with gold and copper brought by the Beaker people from continental Europe, and the alchemy of forging bronze from raw stone ore. Yet I also learnt to remember how even though those eras were defined by metals, stone was still very much in daily use. Flint especially remained an essential material. Agricultural revolutions burnt more slowly. The steady shift to farming – forging the first fields, sowing crops and keeping animals – that was practised by our distant ancestors took many generations to truly embed. The early agriculturalists still hunted and gathered to survive.

And then there were the Romans. Their arrival on these shores brought many changes. The arrival of the written word in Britain officially ended the era of prehistory in these isles. I knew that. But I learnt, too, that the fall of Roman feet on British soils brought no sudden shift in the ways and sensibilities of most British people.

In *Ancient Wonderings*, I perpetually sought to peer over the shoulders of those whose work filters our understanding of the ancient world. So I read the academic papers and books of leading archaeologists and scientists. I met them and listened to them as they spoke about their work. Their precision and patience has refined our vision of how British people lived and died and were buried and remembered in prehistoric times. I learnt by going to the places where the ancient past was still most visible and then tucking down away from the present world and digging down within, digging inside to realise what it is, what it has ever been, to be human. That process involved becoming immersed into a landscape, spending time in that world by day and by night – walking the terrain, getting to know the lie of the land: the geography, the geomorphology and the geology. To know a place you must start local – by reading its literatures and histories, listening to the voices of its peoples – steadily building an understanding and knowledge of a specific landscape, gradually unearthing a deeper topography. Then, and only really then, can you hope to venture back in time to try to see how that environment might once have looked. And only then can you begin to imagine the people and their ancient practices in that place so many years ago. It was at such times that I saw clearest – flowing through deepest time, seeking to see into the ways of past generations.

James Canton
March 2017

an illegible stone ...
that is where we start.

T. S. Eliot, 'Little Gidding'
Four Quartets

STONE

I had fallen under the spell of a stone. It was in May half-term that I found a window from teaching. To find that stone I would venture to the north-east of Scotland and so I headed north until I reached the town of Insch.

Yet I had no map. When I asked where I might find one, the two women in the chemist's looked to each other. They could have been twins. Both had short grey hair and glasses. Their faces were round and friendly. Had I tried the DIY store? I had. What about the post office? I had tried that, too. They smiled.

'Mmm,' they both said.

Then one spoke.

'What about the garden centre just down the road. They might have one.'

'Ay, they might,' echoed the other.

The day was grey. I walked to the edge of the town where a new housing estate was rising from the earth and then for two miles more along the B992, skipping from the tarmac of the road to the grassy bank each minute or so as a car whooshed past. A buzzard circled above. In a copse of spruce trees an incessant mewing told of young buzzard chicks. I continued to dodge the sporadic traffic and soon reached the A96 with the choice to walk north to Inverness or south, back to Aberdeen. Instead, I turned down the slip road to the Kellockbank Country Emporium. The ladies from the chemist were right. By the bars of chocolate and racks of magazines, lay just what I wanted: Ordnance Survey Explorer maps 420 and 421.

There I stood. I had travelled some five hundred miles to this windswept place in Northern Scotland, beside an A-road some twenty miles north-east of Aberdeen. I was there to see a stone – a standing stone; a stone that held a story. The only problem was that there was a locked gate between me and the stone and I didn't have a key.

The tale of that stone had been lodged for years, tucked away. Every once in a while the knowledge would work its way to the surface of my thoughts. Then, I would find a way to tell the tale:

'There is a stone in Scotland …' the story would begin.

About a year ago, I had found myself in the Rare Books reading room of the British Library in London, sometime in the afternoon of a warm day in May, and rather drifting away from the research I was meant to be undertaking on an explorer of the Arabian desert. Thoughts of that stone had arrived unexpectedly in my mind. I had ordered up some books on what I remembered was called the Newton Stone.

The facts were simple: the Newton Stone was a block of granite, or rather blue gneiss, something over six feet from top to toe on which there are carved two inscriptions. One is in Ogham script – a Celtic writing system that appears as a series of scratch-like marks torn into the side of the stone. A second, more prominent, script is engraved into the face of the stone consisting of six roughly horizontal lines of writing. Each line consists of some form of exotic lettering from an ancient language: a series of swirls, curves and curlicues carved into the surface of this mass of granite. What those letters say remains a mystery. That text has yet to be deciphered.

It seemed unbelievable that there could be a piece of written script sat on British soil that no one in the world could understand. There, in that hub of all known knowledge – in London, in the British Library – I gazed incredulous that those simple lines of script before me held a message which all our centuries of collective study had been unable to fathom.

A week on, I sat at home in my study. The Royal Commission on Ancient and Historical Monuments of Scotland website simply stated that:

> The ogam-inscribed stone (The 'Newton Stone') is of blue gneiss, 2.03 m x 0.5 m, and bears at the top six horizontal lines of characters and an ogam-inscription down the left angle and lower front of the stone.

No indication of mystery there. A second monument that sits alongside the Newton Stone was described as a Pictish symbol stone. The stones were in the garden of Newton House, some twenty miles north-west of Aberdeen. I rang Historic Scotland.

'We can't give out owner details,' said the woman from the scheduling department.

She suggested I try calling the post office in the nearest village. I rang Old Rayne Post Office and elderly lady with a soft Scottish accent answered.

'I'm afraid we're not a post office any more,' she said.

She suggested I rang the Old School House. I did. Another softly spoken voice told me to try Old Rayne Community Association.

'They'll know.'

I found their number and left a message on their answer machine. It wasn't going well.

Then I received an email from Sally Foster. She was an archaeologist at the University of Aberdeen who I had contacted asking for advice on the Newton Stone.

Dear James

I'm afraid that I don't know how to contact the owners, other than to write to the occupiers of the house. Historic Scotland's scheduling team will have full details because the monument is scheduled.

I'm dashing for a train now and will return to your question about best sources for latest thinking when I get back next week.

All the best for now.

Sally

She remained good to her word. A week later, a second email offered a list of reading and an intriguing lead:

My colleague Professor David Dumville has some new but

unpublished ideas about one of the Newton stones, so I am
copying him into this.

I emailed Professor Dumville immediately. Then I turned
back to Newton House. Surely it was possible to find a
phone number. I rang directory enquiries. A young Indian
voice answered.

'What is the name you are seeking, please?'

'Newton House, please.'

'Business or residential?'

'Erm ... residential.'

'And the name?'

I hesitated; confessed I knew no more.

'I need information to find the number,' she stated.

She was fast, efficient: New World. I pictured her in a call
centre in Bangalore. I was slow, blithering: Old World. I
thanked her and hung up.

Two weeks on, there was still no reply from Professor
Dumville. I emailed him again and then rang the archaeology department at Aberdeen.

'He'll be back next week,' a voice informed me.

The following week I tried again. No answer. I tried a
second email address. An online search had come up
with a phone number for what seemed a fishery based at
Newton House. The phone rang for an age. Finally, a woman

answered. I said I was trying to visit the Newton Stone and wanted to speak to the owners of Newton House.

'The big house,' she said. 'I don't know the name of the people.'

She sounded nervous.

'They're not local,' she added.

I asked how I might get to see the stone.

'The house is just off the A96,' she said. 'Ask at the security gate for them to let you in.'

Now, I stood at the gate. Here was the moment of truth. I rang the buzzer and listened intently beneath the swoosh of cars on the main road a few feet away. There was no answer. I pressed another button on the keypad and there was a faint ringing tone like a distant telephone. It stopped.

There was a pause. A silence that lasted too long. Then nothing.

'Hello?' I asked.

I pressed the button again. The ringing tone started up again.

'Hello,' a voice said cheerfully.

'Oh, hello,' I said. 'I spoke to a lady a while ago about coming to see the Newton Stone.'

There was another silence.

'Hello?' I said again.

A long tone rang out through the speaker. The gate shifted, squeaked rustily.

'Come in,' said the woman's voice.

Magically, the gate began to slowly open before me. I stepped forward.

The gate opened on to a path, which wound down a soft incline into another world that seemed as though a kind of paradise. Birdsong rang out. A flycatcher flitted about in the still bare outer branches of a beech tree. The path led to the edge of a stream. On the far bank the skeletal remains of last year's giant hogweed stood tall among this year's wide young fronds – their broken frames fragile, delicate and leaning rather a-kilter. A beech hedge ran to my right. A line of broad-leafed limes ran beside the riverbank. I crossed a bridge over the river, pausing inevitably over the water before proceeding. An avenue opened before me, formed from the leaves, the branches of beech trees, which produced a distant focal point to which I slowly headed.

Newton House stood beautifully positioned before me. It was Georgian square, stately and solid beside a pea-shingle driveway. A small, rectangular sign stated 'Newton Stones' and pointed past the house to a smaller pathway of pale gravel, edged with sections of beech hedge that wove into woodland. Deep green rhododendron bushes bunched out into the spaces left by Douglas fir that reached high above – their bare lower trunks wonderfully sinewed. Over the ground lay a copper brush of last year's beech leaves that soon transformed to a carpet of pink campion. The path ended.

There were two standing stones. Each stood two metres tall; each was topped with a wig of soft, green moss. Posies of yellow primrose had been planted about the stones. To the side, there was a white, metal-framed bench and a table in the form of a slab of slate resting on foot-high sections of beech trunk. For a moment I did not know quite what to do. Here before me was the Newton Stone. Here was the strange script.

I stepped closer, reached out a hand and touched the granite with my forefinger, stroked the edge of the stone as though it were some wild animal that needed greeting, gentle reassurance I was friend not foe. There was nothing of the coldness to the touch that I had anticipated.

I stepped away. The stone was the colour of cloud. In places, the surface of the stone was patched of whiter, paler shades formed by some long Latin-named lichen. The Ogham script was easily made out: a series of engraved lines, each two, three inches long; each close to horizontal and running parallel down the edge of the stone. The script appeared as a line of scars, a tribal marking that ran the length of one side of the stone. To the trained eye, these lines in the stone were far less controversial. They now made sense; they could be read. On the front of the stone was the undeciphered writing. I stared. There seemed a sinuous sense to much of the script. The letters looked as though they flowed together naturally enough and yet here before me were words that the greatest minds could not fathom, that not the wisest archaeologists or philologists, the most esteemed professors of linguistics, could make head nor tail of. There was the fylfot, the mark in the centre of the engraving: a swastika by any other name. Yet that symbol meant something so much more sinister to our modern eyes. To pre-twentieth-century eyes, the pattern was one formed by four Greek symbols: four capital Gamma signs placed together – a gammadion.

I peered at the first line of script. The initial letter looked like a lopsided C. Then an I. Then two Fs? I stopped. I had done all this before to photographs of the script. I leaned my head to the side a little. Did the script run from left to right or from right to left? I reached forward, traced each letter with my finger, then leaned my head closer, starring into the fissures of the carving.

Between the two stones, secured into the ground was a metal plaque. I brushed the bosky detritus of beech leaves and twigs away to reveal the following words:

The enigmatic carved stones are not in their original position. The symbol stone bearing a double-disc and a serpent and Z-rod is Pictish. The other stone bears Oghams – a Celtic alphabet along its side and an inscription in a different alphabet on its face. Readings of these two inscriptions are a subject of controversy.

This monument is protected as a monument of national importance under the AM Acts of 1913–53.

– Secretary of State for Scotland

On the second stone, far easier to make out, were two distinctive symbol markings: the snaking pattern of a serpent-figure, and above the double circles of a second, stranger sign.

I walked away and sat on the metal bench.

It was a beautiful setting. Mixed woodland. Beech, Douglas fir. Bluebells. Birdsong. Whitethroat and chaffinch calling. I sat and ate my lunch. There was something gloriously reassuring in that quotidian task of eating, of stepping away from the solemn presence of that standing stone a few feet before me and those illegible six lines carved across its chest. I listened to the birdsong, glanced about me at this picnic spot and then remembered: it was a folly; nothing more than an imagined site, a constructed landscape: a glade in the wood – the ancient stones framed by a beech hedge; the primula; the bench and the slate table. I laughed out loud at the ease with which a few accoutrements can create a sense of solemnity. I was sitting in a Victorian grotto.

For this was not the original site of the Newton Stone. The stone had been discovered by shepherds back in 1803 half a mile or so south on the side of a hill overlooking Shevock Burn. The stone had been brought here in 1837 and placed in the present position in 1873 as the perfect Victorian garden orna-ment – an ancient monument with unexplained inscriptions. Not that there weren't learned antiquarian gentlemen already offering their theories. I had trawled the British Library. Only sixty years after the Newton Stone was unearthed there was already excited speculation. Writing in the *Proceedings of the Society of Antiquaries of Scotland*, Alexander Thomson of Banchory noted with a certain evident pride how:

> It is provoking to have an inscription in our own country of unquestionable genuineness and antiquity, which up to this time, seems to have baffled all attempts to decipher it.

That was in 1863. Conjecture flourished. The eminent 'Dr Mill of Cambridge, one of the most profound oriental schol-ars of the day' saw the inscription as 'in the old Phoenician character and language'.

I took a bite of my sandwich and looked back to those six lines of inscription then rose and returned to the stone, touched again the rough edges of that first letter, the lopsided C. The same questions swirled. Who had made these words? What did they say? Who were they carved for? Who was meant to read them?

Even to my ill-tutored eye there seemed something distinctly Oriental in the swirls and whirls of the lettering. The Phoenician theory was one that had held for a good while. L. A. Waddell was a Victorian antiquarian and linguist whose elaborately entitled work *The Phoenician origin of Britons, Scots and Anglo-Saxons: Discovered by Phoenician and Sumerian Inscriptions in Britain, by pre-Roman Briton Coins and a mass of new History* had first been published in 1924. Waddell claimed not only to have deciphered and translated the Newton Stone script – which he dated to 400 BC – but saw the monument as evidence of Phoenician colonists who were the ancestors of the ancient Britons.

I rather liked the notion of Phoenicians reaching the north of Scotland on one of their expeditionary trading missions and their decision to stay, to settle here. It was a fanciful one, of course. I mused a moment on Waddell's theory, sat there beside the stone, and imagined a young Phoenician traveller who falls in love with a local lass. He will stay, he declares. He cannot leave. Time passes. He prospers, grows old. He has spent a lifetime here. He prepares for his final journey, the one to the undiscovered country. He commands a stonemason to carve a message into one of the vast standing stones. He remembers pieces, fragments of his native language.

It was time I moved on. I packed up the picnic and placed my hand on the stone. It was an odd gesture, I thought later, and yet I did so automatically all the same, as though touching the shoulder of a friend in farewell. The pale gravel pathway continued on through gladed woodland. The map had shown a track running down from the grounds of Newton House, from what were referred to as 'Sculptured Stones', away south through open fields to further woodland, running directly to the original site of the stone. Strangely, the map also indicated the track would pass a mausoleum within the grounds.

It was while on the trail of the Newton Stone, tucked away in the recesses of the British Library, that I had discovered John Buchan's *The Watcher by the Threshold.* * The work was a collection of stories first published in 1902 and all set in Scotland. In a dedication to his friend Stair Agnew Gillon, Buchan stated:

---

* John Buchan, *The Watcher by the Threshold and Other Tales* [1902] (London: Nelson and Sons, 1922)

It is of the back-world of Scotland that I write, the land behind the mist and over the seven bens, a place hard of access for the foot-passenger but easy for the maker of stories. Meantime, to you, who have chosen the better part, I wish many bright days by hill and loch in the summers to come.

J. B.

R.M.S. Briton, at sea

September 1901

It was the first of the stories – 'No-Man's Land' – that most intrigued. Buchan's tale tells the sad fate of a young Oxford academic, an archaeologist called Mr Graves, who is holiday-ing in his Scottish homeland. Graves is entranced by the Picts:

> They had troubled me in all my studies, a sort of blank wall to put an end to speculation. We knew nothing of them save certain strange names which men called Pictish, the names of those hills in front of me – the Muneraw, the Yirnie, the Calmarton. They were the *corpus vile* for learned experiment; but heaven alone knew what dark abyss of savagery once yawned in the midst of this desert.

Graves tells of his own journey into the heart of this land-scape. He meets an old shepherd and his wife who talk of lost lambs, of sheep found dead with a hole in their throats.

Graves laughs at mention of the Brownie – those mythical, half-forgotten beings; shrunken, ancient men who were said to still live in the wildest spaces of the moors. He heads out for a place called the Scarts of the Muneraw:

> … in the hollow trough of mist before me, where things could still be half discerned, there appeared a figure. It was little and squat and dark; naked, apparently, but so rough with hair that it wore the appearance of a skin-covered being.

Graves has met the Brownie – those remnants of the still-surviving Picts. He flees in terror but is chased, bundled to the ground and knocked unconscious.

I had paused my reading to check up on the Picts. They were a people of north and eastern Scotland dating from pre-Roman times until the eleventh century or so when they merged with the Gaels. These were Buchan's Brownies. Then I had rung Professor Dumville's phone number again.

'The number you have dialled has not been recognised. Please check and try again.'

I had been expecting a Scottish voice to answer. Instead the recording was oddly clipped – the Standard English of an imperial English voice from a century ago – in fact, a voice rather well suited to a figure like Buchan's Oxford academic Mr Graves. Professor Dumville seemed to have vanished from all possible communication. I rang the main university switchboard. The operator tried the number. The same imperial English voice answered.

'Yeah, that's very strange,' she agreed in a Scottish tone. 'I'll report it to the engineers.'

In the meantime, she put me through to the Department of Archaeology's general office. I left another message then returned to 'No-Man's Land'.

Graves wakes to find himself 'in a great dark place with a glow of dull firelight in the middle'. He gathers his courage and speaks in dimly recalled Gaelic. A tribal elder from the back of the cave stumbles forward: 'He was like some foul grey badger, his red eyes sightless, and his hands trembling on a stump of bog oak.' The old man speaks. Graves is spellbound:

For a little an insatiable curiosity, the ardour of the scholar, prevailed. I forgot the horror of the place, and thought only of the fact that here before me was the greatest find that scholarship had ever made.

Graves hears of the survival of the Picts – of girls stolen from the lowlands, of 'bestial murders in lonely cottages'. Then he escapes. He flies from the hill cavern and from Scotland, back to the cloisters of St Chad's, Oxford where he burns all books, all references to the moorlands. But, of course, Graves is tortured by the knowledge he now holds. Reluctantly, he returns to the Muneraw and finds himself once more in that hidden hillside where now a young local woman is being prepared for sacrifice. Graves fires on these strange ancient relics of men and flees with their captive. A final struggle on the edge of a ravine sees one of the remaining Picts fall 'headlong into the impenetrable darkness'. Graves is badly injured; dazed, but still alive.

There the narrative breaks. The last chapter of 'No-Man's Land' is told by an unnamed editor. Graves' words were written before he died of heart failure. An obituary notice in *The Times* is quoted which remembers the great potential Graves showed as an archaeologist, though tempered with the caveat that:

> He was led into fantastic speculations; and when he found himself unable to convince his colleagues, he gradually retired into himself, and lived practically a hermit's life till his death. His career, thus broken short, is a sad instance of the fascination which the recondite and the quack can exercise even over men of approved ability.

I stepped away from the stones yet was loathe to leave. In the woodland, the extraordinary song of a tree pipit reverberated bold and fluid as a Highland stream, rattling and ranting over the low cover of creeping ivy and floods of pink campion.

The track left the trees and followed the line of the River Kellock to a sheep field that had been fenced off. I stepped gingerly over, scattering sheep up the hillside towards the incongruous and faintly unnerving sounds of traffic coming from the nearby A96. I held close to the Kellock. A farm track carved by tractor wheels ran beside the riverbank, which was smothered with the triffid-like leaves of hogweed. I glanced at the map where the track marks ran straight to the original site of the stone. Before me was more barbed wire. Beyond, through a copse of trees, I could make out a building of some sort. I followed the farm track, down to the flood plain of the river. The stones had been described as being in a plantation near the Shevock toll-bar. This was the raised triangle of land I now stood before. I looked about. Three crows flew by. Sheep stared. I tried to picture the stones earthfast on the embankment above. South ran the valley of the River Shevock; north rose the dark Hill of Rothmaise. This was no place to linger. I felt it. Something was hurrying me away. I was standing on someone else's land. The enclosed copse with the smallholding felt full of shadows. I looked back to the map and traced the snaking, red line of the A96. I had circled in pencil the stone circle on Candle Hill past Old Rayne. I turned back to the land. Barbed-wire fencing surrounded. I walked on heedless, away from the copse until the Shevock blocked my path, then lurched ungainly over a section of fencing and clambered up towards the road.

Past Pitmachie, I crossed the bridge over the Shevock and wove into the village of Old Rayne, up past the market cross where a line of schoolchildren snaked downhill as I went up, climbing the inclines to Candle Hill where a starling greeted my arrival from the rooftop of an abandoned farm shed. I sat on one of the fallen outliers of the stone circle. The clouds of earlier were clearing. A breeze blew. There was blue sky to the north over Gartly Moor and the Hill of Foudland. I gazed back and could make out that triangular embankment of raised land, the original site of the stone.

The belief that the Newton Stone had been carved in that strange script as some form of memorial was one that had held strong since the modern unearthing at the start of the nineteenth century. There was a logic in seeing a funereal nature to the engraving; that the stone had been a gravestone and the words an epitaph. Certainly, that was what I had assumed. In a paper published in 1882, the Earl of Southesk – the writer offered no other name – had noted that when 'trenching' of the Shevock area had taken place around 1,837 human bones had been found 'a few yards' from the original site of the Newton Stone. On the sleeper train up to Aberdeen, with notions of the Newton Stone and its enigmatic engraving playing along to the motion of the

22

tracks, I had tucked down to sleep and begun to imagine that I was indeed one of the dead and was in fact lying in a sarcophagus of some sort, starting on that journey to the next world, the narrow bunk bed and the low roof helping to frame my fanciful thoughts. I placed my most valuable possessions about me, in the soft edges of the upper bunk, as though they were some form of modern grave goods – items that I would need in my next life: iPod, mobile phone, torch, glasses, and wallet.

When I stepped from the stone circle on Candle Hill two wagtails mobbed me, fluttering about my head. The open road ran south down the hill. Two goldfinches flew along-side, rested a while on a fence wire as the sun broke out from behind cloud, their black and red striped hoops reminding me of coral snakes. At Strathorn Farm, an old boy sat high in a tractor, slowly raised a hand and reversed. A heap of metal detritus was piled about the farm sheds in that way some old farmers have of simply dumping unwanted goods all out in the open: a lawn mower; a Flymo with fading 1970s orange; bits of metal pipes twisted to tortuous angles; a rusting washing machine; discarded gas canisters. A collection of waste, all weathering slowly away, seeping back to their residual minerals, metals. I thought too of the sense that though I now walked this ancient roadway boldly towards three Pictish stones planted somewhere over the wooded horizon, that I too in time would slowly weather back to my residual parts, until my calcareous deposits too would leach and litter the land.

I wandered on towards the Elphinstone estate. Two oystercatchers stood upon red-tinged clods. A yellowhammer called from a phone wire. Down a hawthorn-lined lane in the estate lands, a miasma of St Mark's flies filled the air such that I was forced to walk along through a cloud of long, shiny, black bodies, each one dangling dark legs that hung as though paralysed from the fly's torso. The religiosity in naming these creatures after St Mark supposedly comes from their emergence close to the saint's day of 25 April, and yet the manner in which each fly flew with wings wide and pendulous legs dangling reminded of a shrunken dark cross, a crucifix. I pictured St Mark being dragged about the streets of Alexandria, a rope tied about his neck, his black-robes hanging dirty about his lifeless form, and wondered if this image wasn't the inspiration for the beatification of these flies by Carl Linnaeus when he had named them *Bibio marci* in his tenth edition of the *Systema Naturae* back in 1758.

The flies vanished. I stepped back into woodland where the bare pine carpet was littered with tiny, bright green posies that were bunches of new growth snipped from the higher branches of the pines by the flocks of finches and that now lay like votive offerings – minute nosegays or scattered sea anemones lost in the woods. Each was perfectly soft to the touch, the young needles in gentle clumps, the severed attachment turning brown in the air. I picked several from the floor, some truly no bigger than an agate stone, smelt each one, and put them into my shirt pocket. When I found them later that day they had already lost their soft lustre.

By Logie Elphinstone House I found the three symbol stones. The setting was stunningly elegiac. I sat on the bare earth, sheltered under a canopy of elephantine-limbed beech trees, surrounded with sprays of bluebells interspersed with the pale heads of albino-white variants and the dying embers of daffodils. A single red tulip burnt crimson like a dying sun. In the peace of that space I massaged my aching feet and watched two tree creepers flit from one huge beech trunk to the moss and lichen cover of another. On the stones there were those strange symbols that told the archaeologists they were Pictish. Each was half the size of the Newton Stone. They had been found in 1812 when the nearby Moor of Carden was planted. Later that century, they had been placed with due reverence in this setting. A line of shrunken tombstones had been added. These stone lozenges, each perhaps nine inches across and a foot and half tall, each bore the name of faithful pets – dogs, I assumed.

Wee White	Lady
1919	1918
1929	1926

Fitting with the notion of a place of the dead, the sense naturally emerged that beneath each of the three larger Pictish symbol stones there lay too the body of some brave and loyal being. These stones had various lifetimes, various roles not only for separate generations but for separate eras of human existence on this land, for distinct and different peoples. In the short time since they had been prised from the peat in 1812, these three stones had served as sections of wall in the plantation boundary and then later as some form of mock burial markers in an Edwardian pet cemetery. I wondered how long they had lain upon the Moor of Carden. Had they been carved there or elsewhere? With these wondrous whirls and circles, these sceptre lines so straight, these crescent curves of a moon, the symbols were mesmerising. I thought back to the Newton Stone, to the turns and curls of the script that I had travelled all these miles to see. How many times had the Newton Stone been moved about these lands? How many hands had sat and touched that hard stone and prepared to etch into its dark surface their own lines, the messages of their peoples?

These stones were reused across time. Perhaps these stones were picked out as they had stood as the chief standing stones in the stone circles that ringed the hilltops of the lands, those Candle Hills where fires burnt furiously on sacral days and nights. The Newton Stone had first been raised from the soil for its shape, its size, its standing. Then many, many generations later, the stone had been selected again, to be shifted, brought down a hillside to begin a new existence: the rebirthing of the Newton Stone as a surface for scripture; in time a palimpsest to three forms of script, three formal writing systems, each carved across the body of the stone. Here was the journey from an existence of preliterate sacred significance to becoming a literary landscape, an inscribed monument. Beside those three Pictish stones, I lay back against the soil, closed my eyes to the fractured light of the beech leaf canopy, and stretched my bare feet out into the cold, cooling leaves of bluebells. I thought of the hands that carved those lines, sought Buchan's strange shrunken men.

I returned to Insch along the B9002. A steady line of passing cars told of commuters back from Aberdeen. At the modern ruins of the Archaeolink Prehistory Park weeds rose from an empty car park and a sign in the smart, new, glass-fronted bunker building told the site had been abandoned due to lack of funding. I paused and looked north across the railway line to where my map told of further sites: another Candle Hill rose beside a series of fine black dots marked *Stone Circle* and an outlying single dot labelled *Standing Stone*. More vast stone markers hauled and framed into the landscape by peoples long forgotten. I had already passed a sign to the Maiden Stone back on the turning to Garioch. Yet none of these neighbouring stones held that same cursive script as the Newton Stone.

I walked on. On a bridge over the railway line I stared west and suddenly noticed that in the sky a series of inky black streams of cloud now rested over the land like vast dark sheets or veils formed of gossamer thin threads that seemed to waver in the air. I had never seen anything like them before. The clouds – for these dark waves could be nothing but – appeared to be formed from translucent silk shrouds that were falling gently from the sky. The single, dark body of a crow flew beneath while beyond the sky was pale blue with banks of foaming white cloud like seahorses rising from the waves of an incoming Atlantic storm. I found myself transfixed by these strange cloths of cloud which were certainly made more dramatic that afternoon as they lay above and seemed to mimic the flowing motion of the hills below and where in the distance I could clearly make out the Gothic ruins of Dunnideer Castle, the remains of a thirteenth-century fort that sat on the highest hillside over-looking Insch and consisted of what appeared to be a single triumphal arch, a window of light framed by stone – an ancient solitary dolmen.

When I returned to the Commercial Hotel in Insch, I climbed the three flights of unstable stairs to my rooftop room. I lay on the bed and when I woke after a short sleep it was to find that soot-fingered dusk was finally falling on the day. Through the skylight in the bathroom it looked as though the world was on fire. I opened the window in the roof and gazed south towards the Garioch Hills where it seemed an inferno was burning beyond the still green hillsides and as if the flaming embers of those furious fires were reaching up to the sky, for the undersides of the clouds blazed with unholy colour, blushed as they were with an incredibly unnatural and bloody hue; deep shades of fiery reds, incarnadine and darkening with every second that I stood and gazed.

The following day I was due to meet Sally Foster in Aberdeen. She had assured me the mysterious Professor Dumville would be there too. Yet there were still sites around Insch to see. As I packed, I juggled the options. I would march to the Picardy Stone – another classic Pictish symbol stone two miles or so north. The map was splayed on the bed. The neighbouring hillside was labelled as another Candle Hill topped with a stone circle: if there was time I would nip up the Hill of Dunnideer, get a close up of that strange Gothic arch.

Past the edges of Insch, the road north rose steadily, flat and empty. I walked at marching pace. There were the remains of another stone circle on the hillside west. I headed on. The road fell into a dell where birdsong blew over me from a sheltered glade soft as cherry blossom. I did not halt but strode on down a perfect avenue of beech trees which reminded me of the passageway towards Newton House the day before and which, even in the clear light of that morning, held a strangely sinister sense, an oddly tangible touch of malevolence that I could only trace to a feeling induced by the emptiness of the road, the overarching, enclosing nature of the beech trees as they framed the way ahead, funnelling me towards a distant vanishing point. I passed a sign pointing to the Leys of Largie. The Picardy Stone appeared in the edge of a green field between two beech trunks, coloured the same tone of grey as the trees. I stumbled over the stile. The stone had been encaged. I stepped into its enclosure, touched its shoulder. There were some of those same Pictish symbols carved on the body of the stone: a serpentine shape; two elaborate circles or discoid figures; and the outline of what looked like a hand mirror. An information board for Historic Scotland stated:

Welcome to the Picardy Symbol Stone

A Place of Burial

Beneath this Pictish symbol stone are the remains of a small burial cairn, probably erected 1,300–1,500 years ago. An empty grave-shaped pit was found under one side of it.

On the grey stone stile, I balanced a cup of Thermos tea. A still had descended. The winds had died. I glanced up towards the heights of another Candle Hill, then over to the Hill of Dunnideer. There would be no time to climb either. The Picardy Stone was within view of both. Was that significant? The Newton Stone – even at its earlier setting where it was found in 1804 – was on low ground. It could be seen from the high points but was sited where people actually lived. You wouldn't live on the hilltops. You might head there for special occasions. Yet the symbol stones and the Newton Stones were on the low ground. They were placed for daily viewing. You didn't bury the dead on the high ground. You went up there on specific, special occasions. To speak to the Gods. To celebrate and to appease.

I touched the Picardy Stone a final time, stepped over the stile down to the road. What of those Pictish symbols? I thought of a carved, wooden figure I had at home that my daughter Eva had loved to hold when she was only a toddler and which still rested on her bookshelves. It was a Buddhist statue I had bought from a street trader in north-eastern India many years before of a man sat cross-legged, in the lotus position, meditating. In his hand he held a hand mirror to see the reflection of his soul. That mirror and the symbol on the stone seemed remarkably similar. I walked on, strolling now back down the avenue of beech trees. So what was I saying? That there were Buddhist links to the Picts? I was heading down the same road as those Victorian antiquarians of the past who had seen Phoenician in the Newton Stone script, who had traced an Eastern ancestry for the ancient people of Britain. It was easy enough to do.

In the wide field beyond the beeches parallel ridges ran through the red, iron-rich soil. Three tractors traced the lines. Passing here earlier I had seen a lone farmer pushing single potatoes into the topsoil of a drill: stooping and rising; stooping again. And though he had surely only been testing the depth to set the tractor to, I had immediately thought of that learnt motion of labour, that mechanical precision built into muscle and passed down through time, generation to generation until our time when those patterns of history were splayed and broken. I thought too of the words of Seamus Heaney's 'At a Potato Digging' where:

Centuries
Of fear and homage to the famine god
Toughen the muscles behind their humbled knees,
Make a seasonal altar of the sod.*

---

* Seamus Heaney, *Death of a Naturalist* (London: Faber, 1966), p. 31.

We no longer worshipped at that altar; no longer knew that fear. We had come so far from those days. I wondered, as I wound back to Insch, whether it was indeed still possible to step into the feelings, into the thoughts, the fears, hungers and desires of our ancestors, of those people who lived here one thousand, two thousand years before.

A yellowhammer was sat on a post singing his song. I walked past only feet away.

'Please stay,' I whispered under my breath.

His head turned. I do not know if he heard me but he did stay. On the rise of the hill heading back into Insch, I looked east across to where the Newton Stone lay, made out the Matchbox cars and lorries criss-crossing on the A96. The buzzard was there; tracing widening circles in the sky. Below, on the roadside I could make out the copse of three pine trees, their dark-topped canopy and from that distant place heard the pale cries of those buzzard chicks though only the wind blew about me.

When I met Sally Foster later that day in Aberdeen her office floor was patterned with sets of third-year archaeology exam papers laid out like pale gravestones. Sally sat serenely at her desk amid the layers of paper.

'So you did get to see the stone?' she asked with a smile.

She knew of the difficulties of getting to the site. I told of clambering over barbed-wire fences to the original site of the stones on Shevock. Sally laughed.

'I'm really sorry,' she said. 'Professor Dumville *was* due to join us, but he's had to leave for Liverpool.'

I started to wonder if he really existed.

'He sent his apologies,' added Sally as though reading my thoughts. She picked a card off the table. 'And he's given me his mobile number for you to call.'

At lunch we picked over ideas on Pictish stones.

'They're unshaped, previously used,' Sally said.

The notion of multiple lives for these ancient blocks held such practical sense. At first they were hauled to become standing-stone monuments. The inscriptions on the Newton Stone could easily reflect different periods of time entirely; separate carvings holding distinct meanings and senses for different generations, for different peoples living in that same landscape.

Sally had to return to her marking.

'You must have a look at the cathedral,' she said. 'There's even a gravestone inscribed with Ogham – a professor of mathematics, I think.'

She drew directions to where the Ogham gravestone would be. Her detailed directions were like a tiny treasure map. I thanked her again and headed off through the cobbled medieval alleyways, wandering through the botanical gardens before finding myself at the biological sciences department where the bones of a blue whale filled one wall.

The cathedral of St Machar was perfectly solid and squat, the granite frame appearing resistible to all forces: an apparently everlasting monument. Machar had travelled with Columba from Ireland to Iona, carrying Christianity across the treacherous waters of the Irish Sea. Machar was meant to have built a place of worship on this site sometime around 580 AD. I stared at patterns of the heraldic wooden ceiling, at the mosaic web of the stone walls, and thought of the notion of multiple lives for ancient stones like the Newton Stone. It ran true here. In the cathedral graveyard, I followed Sally's map to the modern Ogham in vain, getting happily distracted by the sweet calling of a goldfinch from the summit of a grand elm tree high above the gravestones. The sky was empty; perfectly summer-blue. I stopped and sat. I was surrounded by stones that had been shaped and carved, many placed together to form a place of collective shelter, of worship; many others had been inscribed to memorialise individual lives. It was obvious. This was what we had always done with stone.

On the train south I started to really drift and wonder. That running screen of land and sky, the space the train affords and the motion of easy speed often acts as a conduit that allows thoughts to well and rise. So it was that day. In many ways, though I had reached out and touched the Newton Stone, had stood on the land where it had first been raised, I had got no nearer to answering the mystery of the script.

As we left Aberdeen I watched as the blocks of stone high-rise housing blurred into rocky outcrops patched with sulphurous yellow gorse. Sitting opposite me were a couple that I took to be from Norway. Like me they stared through the window to the drama unfurling: morning mists rolled in the space between sea and land; green fields seemed to fall into a grey void. I listened to their whispered talk, catching their excitement though their words meant nothing.

That morning on the train from Insch, two oil workers, both men in their middle ages, had talked briefly together in a language I did not know before one fell asleep against the windowpane. The other, beside me, had opened his newspaper. The words were constructed of letters that were largely familiar and yet I could not make out their meaning. I had thought then of the matter of translation, of those six lines of script upon the Newton Stone. Who were they intended for? Who was their readership? Why write them unless they are to be read by someone? Then there was another translational matter: the distinction between the person who carved the words into the stone and the person who had devised the script.

I reached up to the luggage rack, pulled down my bag and delved into the mass of papers I was accumulating. In an article titled 'Literacy in Pictland' by Katherine Forsyth, I found the passage I was after. Forsyth delineated three figures in the engraving process: the *scriptor* who 'drafted the text'; the *lapidarius* who actually carved the stone; and the patron who held the final say. Perhaps in the rubbing space between the three some crucial meaning to the inscription had been lost. I caught the eye of the man opposite. We shared a polite smile and both turned back to the spectacle of the landscape slipping beyond the train window. The grey-bricked facade of a building flashed by, bearing the name The Newton Arms before vanishing into the soft blanket of a sea mist, a fret that fell over the coast, blurring the edges between shore and sea, between headlands and nothingness.

Here was another matter that was starting to bother me: seemingly strange coincidences. Or rather, if not coincidences, a building sense of synchronicity, as though there was a singularly calm and fluid motion to life and that I had just managed to sneak a vision of the underlying structures of that truth. I shook my head a little and thought rationally, thought of confirmation bias – the psychological underpinning that makes us see what we want to see, find the facts to support beliefs that ring true to us such that we make the connections that are relevant to us. So The Newton Arms sign springs out from the mist for me but not for anyone else on the 11:25 Aberdeen to London train (except perhaps someone called Newton). On the train up I had been musing on the manner in which as a traveller you seek differences, see the changes in the tint of the soil, the rises in the land, the yellow of the gorse. Yet in reality the variance is rather less than the resemblance: much remains the same – green fields and trees, rectangular houses.

I plugged in my iPod and chose Joanna Newsom whose harp strings seemed fitting. I closed my eyes:

The meadowlark and the chim-choo-ree and the sparrow
Set to the sky in a flying spree, for the sport of the pharaoh …*

I drifted with the music, the mystery of the lyrics, the movement of the train and woke to the sight of a stretch of water opening beyond the windowpane almost too beautiful to bear as sunshine fell upon the shallow bay at Montrose. On my phone there was a shifting digital dot representing the train making its progress over a map of eastern Scotland. The train was now travelling at eighty-five miles per hour; now eighty-six, now eighty-seven. A constantly updating stream of information swarmed silently, invisibly about me.

---

* Joanna Newsom, 'Emily', from *Ys* (Drag City, 2006).

Yet this simple string of letters that I held in my hand, transcribed from a stone where they were carved hundreds of years earlier, remained an enigma.

Sally Foster and I had talked of the process by which it was possible to gaze back into history, to see shifts over time, movements across centuries and too easily to glaze over the fact that these eras are composed of individual lifetimes – those single units of human existence on the earth – each with their own needs, hungers and desires. One person carved these letters into the granite; one other instructed them to do so. I tried to imagine that moment. Two figures beside a standing stone. Did one of them have paper to write on? No. So how did one show the other what to carve? With a stick in the earth? With dye on bark? Scratched on to clay? The translation of those letters from one to another, from *scriptor* to *lapidarius*, was surely where the meaning was lost. If today's brightest minds could find no meaning then there could be none. Or was that just modern arrogance? Maybe the meaning was still there. Maybe we just couldn't see it.

I changed the music, scanning through the familiar albums for an old favourite, finding Bob Dylan's *Desire* and choosing 'One More Cup of Coffee' before settling back as the first chords broke. South of Arbroath the beaches ran wide and empty. I stopped gazing when I heard the line

'Your voice is like a meadowlark'. That coincidence thing was playing games again.

Past Kirkcaldy, past Kinghorn, the North Sea opened revealing an islet peaked with a red and white striped lighthouse. Sunlight splintered from the slate roofs like spray off the waves. In the distance the Forth Bridge looked like a Meccano simulacrum. The Norwegian woman opposite was pointing at the window, whispering heatedly to her husband. Was she talking so quietly because she didn't want others to hear or because she was being polite, a foreigner in a foreign land; the manners of the traveller? I followed her finger and saw the lighthouse. The island was Inchcolm – home for hermits for a thousand years; burial site for Scottish nobles. More bones and stones.

At Edinburgh, a man sat beside me, placing a large plastic box on the table which contained a small black cat. I caught its stare between the frets of the cage. A feral, wild eye met mine. Just before Berwick where Scotland drew to an end we passed by another golf course. Bunkers of yellow sand stood out from a green baize. Ahead I saw a woman was preparing to drive on the raised dais of the tee.

Then something strange happened: she struck the ball just as she appeared adjacent in my window view such that as the train sped on, it did so at exactly the same speed with which the golf ball flew, which meant that for a few still seconds the ball became a silent companion, travelling along through the open airs to fall on the open space of the fairway and come to a halt perfectly framed in my view-point as that woman golfer had been some specks of time earlier. The entire event lasted no more than perhaps six or seven seconds. The sensation of being suddenly immersed in a world that no longer ran on the same lines as it had done a short time before was undeniable. I turned to the black cat. It stared back, held my gaze.

A little while later the train passed on to the bridge that straddled the River Tweed and so I crossed from one country into another. That return into England occurred precisely as the opening bars of a new song opened in my ears; a jangling melody that was soon accompanied by the meandering voice of Polly Jean Harvey warming up:

I live and die
through England.

I listened spellbound. The words rang out to frame a perfectly synchronous moment of travel. The song was 'England'. I stared through the window to yellow sunshine, to a green countryside; to Elysian fields speckled with wild flowers beyond which rolled distant blue waters topped with white horses. An idealised England.

It leaves
sadness.
...
Remedies
never were,
remedies,
not within my reach.
I cannot go on as I am.

The threnody that runs through the heavenly, Arcadian vision of England seen by Wordsworth or Blake or Edward Thomas, ran here too. I stared with watery eyes. The sudden intensity of the moment was unanticipated.

England
...
It leaves a taste,
*a bitter one.**

A few days later, I rang Professor Dumville. An Old School voice answered. I explained who I was and he apologised for

---

* PJ Harvey, 'England' from *Let England Shake* (Island Records, 2011).

not making the Aberdeen meeting. I said I wanted to know his thoughts on the Newton Stone.

'Well, it's certainly acquired a sense of mystery,' he said.

His voice was deep, confident and fully of authority.

'Exemplifies in spades the notion of the Picts being odd.'

Scattered across my desk were various articles collected from Sally Foster beside various other pencilled notes. One piece of paper was labelled 'Ques for DD'. I couldn't find it.

'Thing is, the archaeologists have gone all PC about the Picts,' he continued. He seemed happy enough to talk. I was sure the sheet was somewhere in the pile.

'I was first shown photographs of the stone way back when taking my MLitt, as a graduate. "What is that script?" I'd been asked. "Old Roman cursive," I'd answered. "That's what it is." But then that means it was carved before 300 AD.'

Professor Dumville's words were worth waiting for. His chatty honesty was utterly refreshing.

'If it's not a fake …' he added.

I stopped.

'A fake?' I asked.

I hadn't even questioned the script's authenticity before. I found my sheet. The first question was a good one. Why was it that a recent paper on Pictish stones was using a transliteration of the Newton Stone script from 1922? The answer was simple.

'There's been no modern work done on the stone. The family wouldn't let anyone in to see. It's only been in the last year or so that the house changed hands. The new owners seem rather friendlier. Did you get to see it?'

'Yes,' I said, rather proudly now I knew so few had managed to.

'So what of that work from the 1920s?' I asked. 'Is it all wrong?

'Well, Francis Diack was rather demonised,' said Dumville. 'But now he's starting to be considered. Good starting point, really.'

I asked more on the aspect of the script itself.

'Well, it's been read as Greek, Palmyrine, Phoenician. You name it ...'

'Oh. Waddell,' I said, remembering my research.

'Indeed.'

'So it's not Phoenician?' I asked

'No. It's not. It's old Roman cursive,' he repeated happily. 'It's very useful to tease people with.' He laughed. 'All I can say is my interest was epigraphic. Why would someone put cursive on a monument? Why was someone doing this in AD 300?'

While I tried to fathom this, tried to fit it with all I had read, Professor Dumville had moved on. He talked some more, on the nature of insular script, a Gaelic written form that had emerged out of the new Roman cursive, before returning to the problem of the Newton Stone script.

'There has to be a physical way of explaining the nature of the letters in that scripture,' he explained. 'Such that their age can be properly assessed and a better sense built of when they were carved.'

But no real archaeological study of the stone had taken place for close on a century.

'I suspect it'll turn out to be a fake,' he declared firmly.

Remarkably, *The Newton Stone and other Pictish Inscriptions* by Francis C. Diack (1922) popped up for sale when I searched online under 'Newton Stone'. It was twenty pounds. I bought it immediately and the book arrived two days later carefully wrapped in brown parcel paper. I pushed everything else on my desk aside. The book was really a booklet. It was just sixty-four pages long. Diack began with a familiar description:

> It is a monolith of blue gneiss, rather over six feet high, and bears two inscriptions. One is in ogam letters along one of the edges and part of one of the faces, ogam being the peculiar Celtic alphabet used on early monuments in Ireland. Higher up on the same face is the other, consisting of six lines of Roman letters in cursive of the first three centuries AD.

That tied in perfectly with Dumville's words. I read on.

Diack turned to the meaning of those six lines. They could be divided into two sections. The first three lines read:

ETTE

EVAGAINNIAS

CIGONOVOCOI

 I read on:

It is apparent at once that we have here proper names, and that the monument is, like every other known example of similar age, a sepulchral record, commemorating the name of the person buried there.

It *was* a funereal stone. The first three lines Diack read as, 'Ette, son of Evagainnias, descendent of Cingo, here'. Only the mother's name was given, fitting with the matriarchy practised by the Picts.

The second three lines record the name of another person. Whether they were cut at exactly the same time as the first three must be doubtful, and whether they were by the same hand, though the technique looks the same.

Those second three lines read:

URAELISI

MAQQI

NOVIOGRUTA

Diack read them as meaning, 'The grave of Elisios, son of New Grus.'* The name of New-Grus was another form of reference linked to Pictish matriarchic traditions.

I made a cup of tea.

So if we were to accept Diack's words, the Newton Stone was indeed used as a burial stone, though Professor Dumville reckoned it would turn out to be a fake. I flicked back through my photos of the stone, to the curved lines of the letters and zoomed in until they blurred to grey cloud. They were carved into granite. If the script was a fake, someone had taken a good deal of effort over it. I thought of those early Victorian antiquarians who had apparently found the stone. They had the time. And the money. And perhaps also an imperfect knowledge of cursive Roman.

I drank my tea. There was something else. Something I'd missed. I opened up all the files I had made from the various works I'd read. It wasn't from those nineteenth-century 'Proceedings of the Society of Antiquaries of Scotland'.

---

* Francis C. Diack, *The Newton Stone and other Pictish Inscriptions* (Paisley: Alexander Gardner, 1922), pp. 7–14.

It was more recent. I found it. It was from Iain Fraser's *The Pictish Symbol Stones of Scotland*:

> Recent examination of the [Newton] stone has also identified
> a mirror symbol on one of its lower facets, and the remains of
> a spiral or concentric ovals towards the base of its rear face.[*]

Then there was that third inscription: Pictish symbols carved on the back of the monument. It was yet another reincarnation for that block of blue gneiss, another rebirth for the Newton Stone as a sacred monument. Those six lines of cursive Roman writing that had so entranced with their mystery, their unknowing, were probably nothing more mysterious than the epitaphs to two men whose bodies were once laid in Scottish soils and whose souls had long since flown. The stone had then formed a slate for later generations to carve their deepest thoughts upon. The deeper mystery surely lay in who those peoples were: the Picts. Professor Dumville had called them 'odd'. John Buchan had seen them as shrunken, hairy brutes. No one really knew. Yet inscribed on the Newton Stone were three forms of writing that were all very different, all distinct, and all associated with the Picts.

---

[*]   Iain Fraser, *The Pictish Symbol Stones of Scotland* (Edinburgh: Royal Commission on the Ancient and Historical Monuments of Scotland, 2008), p. 34.

My mind was racing, excited. I started upstairs to my daughter Eva's room, to that wooden Buddhist statue. On the stairs, I remembered Professor Dumville's words from a couple of days ago:

'Of course, you know there's a history of people going loopy studying this,' he had said, laughing again; the sound echoing rather demoniacally down the phone line. He had told stories of two well-known academics who had completely lost their minds in studying Pictish stones.

'There's a curse hanging over this,' Professor Dumville had warned. 'So watch out.'

Eva lay asleep, splayed across her bed, covers merrily askew. I could hear the gentle breath of sleep of my younger daughter Molly in the next room. In the dusky half-darkness, I found the statue and felt the smoothness, the lightness of the wood. The figure was smaller than I remembered and more crudely formed. His legs were crossed in a lotus position. His hands touched on his front and held a mirror that covered much of his chest. There was a pattern on the mirror that I hadn't remembered: woven lines carved into the wood.

Eva snored softly. For a short while, I simply watched her. Then I returned the wooden statue quietly to the bookcase shelf, tucked Eva in and tiptoed down the steep stairs. Someone else could worry about the links between the Picts and Buddhist mirror symbols.

DOGGERLAND

Several months later, I began to become intrigued by a
place that no longer existed. It was an ancient landscape
that now lay far under the North Sea. It was a world called
Doggerland. There were teasing little indicators of this
world. Small pieces of dark brown organic material could
be found on the Norfolk coast that were segments of peat or
wood from the submerged forests and fenlands of Doggerland as it had existed as an environment, a place for people
to live on and call a home thousands of years ago as the last
Ice Age ended.

It was a project that had been stewing quietly away for a while. On my last birthday my old friend Ant had given me a copy of *Submerged Forests* by Clement Reid. The book had been first published in 1913. I had known of the work but never read it. Clement Reid was another of those Victorians who possessed a wonderfully inquisitive sense of discovery. He had studied geology and biology in the mid-nineteenth century when a biblical-based chronological approach to delineating the ancient world still reigned, forcing the history of human activity on the earth into a six-thousand-year period. Charles Darwin's *On the Origin of Species* had been published in 1859. Then there were those emergent theories of geology by figures such as Charles Lyell that had also served to challenge the dating of prehistory centred on biblical interpretation. Yet notions of prehistoric worlds and their human inhabitants had remained constricted by scripture.

In 1913, Clement Reid was near retirement from his position as geologist at the University of Cambridge. *Submerged Forests* was his summary of work on the ancient landscapes of Britain and Europe, on 'Noah's Woods' – those strange remnants of trees from the past found often with fossilised bones of long vanished animals and lumps of earthy peat or 'moorlog', as the local sailors knew this sea peat. These reminders of past forests were dredged from the dark depths along with the bones of the exotic and extinct creatures that had roamed them; not uncommon catches for the fishermen who worked the North Sea. Clement Reid's *Submerged Forests* collated the evidence for a vast plain stretching from the Dogger Bank for miles south where now the waters of the North Sea lay. The book also raised questions way beyond matters of geology as to the nature of that landscape and of the peoples who lived there at the end of the last great Glacial Epoch and settled the lands of an emergent Britain.

Reid's preface to *Submerged Forests* is a perfect statement on the necessity of interdisciplinary study, the need for a renaissance mindset:

> Knowledge cannot be divided into compartments, each given a definite name and allotted to a different student. There are, and always must be, branches of knowledge in which several sciences meet or have an interest, and these are somewhat liable to be neglected. If the following pages arouse an interest in one of the by-ways of science their purpose has been fulfilled.

The obvious difficulty with exploring Doggerland was that it now lay under many metres of cold, dark, rather forbidding sea. At Easter, walking the beach with my daughter Eva seeking small reminders of those submerged forests that existed beneath the waters, I had wondered on the possibility of reaching one of the sandbanks that still rose from the North Sea during a low tide – such as Dogger Bank itself, which Clement Reid saw as the plateau that stood some thirty metres above the northern edge of the vast 'alluvial flat connecting Britain with Holland and Denmark'.[*]

I had checked maps. It would mean a journey of some one hundred kilometres out into the sea. My initial plan had been to sail away into the North Sea and jump out on to the debatable sands of Dogger Bank. It now seemed rather fanciful. I didn't even know how to sail. I had an inflatable canoe. That was it. Even if I could somehow manage to persuade someone to head out into the open sea; even if I reached some semblance of land out there, I would be standing many, many feet above any signs of Doggerland and the people who lived there ten thousand years ago. The plan needed a rethink.

I turned back to the books.

In 1931, a fishing trawler the *Colinda* was sailing along the Norfolk coast between two raised lands known as the Leman and Ower Banks. It was night when the nets were pulled in. Among the usual odd lumps of peat and a few bones, ship's captain Pilgrim E. Lockwood had a single piece

---

[*] Clement Reid, *Submerged Forests* (Cambridge: Cambridge University Press, 2011 [1913]), p. 106; quoted in Bryony Coles, 'Doggerland: A Speculative Survey', *Proceedings of the Prehistoric Society*, 64, 1998, pp. 45–81 (p. 47).

of moorlog some four feet square. Instead of chucking it back into the dark seas, Lockwood decided to split it open with a shovel. His spade struck something solid. Lockwood broke the moorlog apart. Out fell a prehistoric antler harpoon.[*]

The harpoon was some eight and a half inches long. A row of barbs had been carved along one edge; there was a sharpened point and a series of notches presumably to secure fastening to a shaft. You could easily imagine someone strolling the shores of Doggerland at low tide, using the 'harpoon' to spear flatfish or eels. Here was real evidence of life in Doggerland. The *Colinda* harpoon was dated to Mesolithic times, the Middle Stone Age; an era when the populace of Europe were still hunter-gathers. The more settled, sedentary farming ways of the Neolithic had yet to arrive. Mesolithic existence apparently consisted of small groups of people living in extended family units, communities able to move about the landscapes seasonally, travelling the lands from one favoured site to another: for food, for flints and for shelter.

THE MIDDLE STONE AGE.

I tried to picture a band of Mesolithic folk. It was hard to get rid of cartoon images of *The Flintstones* from my mind. Would they really be wearing animal skins? I thought for a moment

---

[*] See Vincent Gaffney, Simon Fitch and David Smith, *Europe's Lost World: The Rediscovery of Doggerland* (York: Council for British Archaeology, 2009), p. 14.

but couldn't imagine anything else they might be able to wrap around themselves more effectively to keep warm. I needed to get to know the people who lived on Doggerland, to understand something of the ways of the Mesolithic, the people of the Stone Age. And so that was why I was headed to the island of Tiree, off the north-west coast of Scotland. I would get to know the Mesolithic first on those isolated islands of the Hebrides – on Tiree and on Coll – where the land still held fragments, echoes of their lives. I would head to those islands for the summer as the Mesolithic peoples had done many years before. Then I would return south to Norfolk to seek Doggerland.

At Sedbergh, in Cumbria, cloud filled the sky. I was stay-ing with my friends Peter and Susan. After a fish-and-chip supper I joined Peter as he walked Crombie, their Border terrier. We walked along Joss Lane, winding gently upwards as our footsteps echoed beside us. At the five-barred gate into the darkness of the moors beyond, Peter and Crombie turned back. I stepped on. The hills of the Howgills were just visible through the darkness. Storms were predicted for tomorrow.

I looked to the skies and saw only clouds. There would be no meteors tonight. The Perseids would flare and shower across a starlit backdrop but they would do so hidden from me. The only distant lights I could see were those of lone homesteads spaced across the river valley below. A stout footpath sign lit by torchlight pointed to Thorn's Lane through a copse of alder and over the waters of Settlebeck Gill into darkness. I would not walk that way tonight. Another sign pointed back down to Joss Lane. I followed, stepping over giant slugs as a wooden gate thudded behind me. Rain started to fall. The heavens opened. Heavy drops, lumps of thunderous rain, broke upon my face as I stared up into the heavens; and as the torch lit that sodden sky, the raindrops transformed into celestial shards. I smiled. Light appeared to be pouring from the sky. There were heavenly sparks for me to watch falling to earth. I sent Katie a text.

'Xx', it simply said.

It was only a year since we had met.

The next day, I said goodbye to Peter and Susan and travelled north.

I reached the island of Tiree in the late afternoon. A horizon of low, grey, rolling clouds lay just above my head. Rain fell. Wind blew. I had driven off the ferry, turned right at a T-junction and headed east until I ran out of road. I had made a pot of tea with my camping gas stove. Now it was getting dark and I had forgotten how to put up the tent. The poles twisted and turned like the legs of some giant tarantula. Eventually the tent took form, sleek and low against the ground. I sat in the car and looked out across the dusk through the rain to the seas of Gunna Sound, the stretch of water between the island of Tiree and the even smaller isle of Gunna. Beyond, a mile or so away, lay another small island: Coll. Beyond that was the far larger island of Mull and further still Oban on the mainland.

Supper bubbled away. An emerald light flashed: a buoy out in water, marking the channel through Gunna Sound. A green light. I thought of Gatsby.

With darkness came more rain; real rain that drummed incessantly on the outer coating of the tent. I read of Mesolithic times by torchlight. Finally, just before midnight, the rain ceased and all I could hear from within my cocoon were the waves beating against the eastern tip of Tiree.

In the morning, I woke, made tea, packed up and drove back down the single track road, past the low-lying sands of Gott Bay and on down the full length of Tiree to the south-western shore and the perfect, mile-wide scimitar curve of Balephuil Bay.

I wandered the flotsam of the high-water mark. There was only a scattering of modern detritus: fishing line, a few pieces of too colourful plastic and segments of ageing rope that had sheared away years ago and wound up here on these lone and level sands. There were pockets, clusters of stones; pebbles worn to spheroids by so many more years of sea and salt. I looked to the western headland of Ceann a' Mhara then back to the east and the peak of Ben Hynish, the highest point on Tiree. The hill was topped with a giant golf ball providing radar coverage for civil aviation way out in the open spaces of the Atlantic Ocean.

Yet I was trying to get into a Mesolithic mindset. In order to know something of Doggerland, I had travelled hundreds of miles in the opposite direction: north, to Scotland and to this idyllic island of the Inner Hebrides some ten miles long and five miles wide at its greatest girth. There was a reason. Tiree and its neighbouring isles of Coll, Mull, Colonsay and Islay have all revealed evidence of Mesolithic life. As the last Ice Age relented some 10,000 years ago, these Hebridean Islands saw the gradual appearance of hunter-gatherer bands in the region. They came to hunt the deer and wild boar that roamed the inner woodlands. They came to gather the foods of the coasts and the rivers: plants, shells, seals and fish. They came too for the flints which they could fashion into axes, blades and arrow points; into smaller tools, awls and scrapers; into microliths, small slithers of flint stone that could be embedded into wooden hafts to create specialist tools to cut and shred vegetables, to scour skin from hides.

At Balephuil Bay, I headed for the dunes and tucked into a sheltered cove, seeking to turn away from the present, to breeze back through thousands of years of human history until I arrived at a time when the sea level was some six metres higher than today and my eyes would seek out not sea litter on the tide mark but the round nodules of flint which would fit cold and clean into my hand. I closed my eyes and felt the winds on my face, heard the regular pounding of the waves. A moment passed. My eyes opened. The beach looked the same. I felt the same. I glanced about. Nothing had changed. I had only been here a day. It would take a little longer to step back thousands of years into past landscapes, into the minds of the Mesolithic.

I had selected two books to bring out with me that day from the travel library housed in a cardboard box in the back of my car. One was *Mesolithic Cultures of Britain* by Susann Palmer. The book consisted of many pages of hand-drawn sketches of artefacts, fragments of flints found in various sites mainly in southern Britain. The other was *To The Islands* by Steven Mithen, which had been fairly recently published and told of Mithen's search for the Mesolithic of the Hebrides. Surely, this really was ideal. I settled to read in the sand dunes.

The timescales were hard to get your head around. The Mesolithic spanned from around 9600 BC through to 4000 BC. The best way to think of the Mesolithic was as a 'period of postglacial hunting and gathering'. Before came the Palaeolithic: a period of time stretching from 2.6 million years ago when humans made a more basic use of stone tools.

After the Mesolithic Age came the Neolithic – delineated by the rise of farming as a way of life which had spread gradually west across Europe from the Near East, first emerging from the fertile plains of the Levant. It signalled a slow end to hunter-gathering.

Humans had only been farming for six thousand years. Before that, *Homo sapiens* had been hunter-gathering for two hundred thousand years. Earlier ancestors had been foraging an existence in Africa for two million years. I read Mithen's conclusion on modern man:

> Consequently, our bodies and brains remain adapted to a hunter-gatherer lifestyle rather than to the sedentary urban existence that is so predominant today – one in which we are detached from the natural world.[*]

I nodded.

I read on and then flicked on through the pages. There was a photo of the very bay I was sitting in: Balephuil. Mithen and his team of archaeologists had been on Tiree. Even better, there was a photo of a site labelled as T1, some-

---

[*] Steven Mithen, *To The Islands* (Isle of Lewis: Two Ravens Press, 2010), pp. 7 & 3.

where here in the dunes of Balephuil, where a prehistoric pebble beach had been exposed by a storm some years back. The site probably dated to the late Mesolithic.

I poured a cup of tea. They were getting closer. All I had to do was to find T1. Then I really could stand on Mesolithic lands. For the rest of the day, I wandered the miles of dunes seeking out T1. The past remained hidden, so I walked the beach scavenging the wrackline before turning to the rock pools on the point where the limpets lived, steadily stepping into the Mesolithic mindset.

In the morning, I woke to find my body was covered in hives: patches of pale, raised skin, with angry red edges, a hand-span width in places. They had begun the day before as though strange insect bites on my legs. Now they had spread, an archipelago of islands had risen on my skin. They didn't itch but they didn't look good either. I needed to see a doctor. Oddly, further reading of Mithen's *To The Islands* had actually directed me towards a local Tiree doctor who held a fascination for all things Mesolithic: Doc Holliday.

I followed a signpost to The Doctor's House down a bumpy track to the doctor's surgery. Doc Holliday was on holiday. I was to wait in the waiting room. A moment later, I was called through to see another doctor who prescribed antihistamine for the hives. I asked of Doc Holliday.

'Ah,' she said with a smile. 'Just ask at the reception when you hand the prescription in.'

The receptionist turned out to be Doc Holliday's wife. I explained how I had heard of him.

'If you're here for the Mesolithic, he'll definitely want to see you,' she said. She smiled and wrote his number on a piece of paper. Then she gave me my medicine. Such was the simple perfection of small-island living.

I sat in the car and opened the sunroof. The sun had come out this morning, banishing the grey. Tiree lay flat and green beneath blue skies. I rang the number. Doc Holliday answered. He had a meeting later but would happily meet me in the local museum at Scarnish in fifteen minutes. Perfect.

Doc Holliday drove up in a red car with a green emergency light on the roof. He wore a light grey suit and sported matching grey beard and glasses. There was a quiet, intense intelligence to him. We sat in the museum and he asked what I was after. I talked of seeking the Mesolithic of Tiree, of linking those people to the peoples of Doggerland. He listened attentively; nodded. He couldn't have been more accommodating. He told me of the Mesolithic sites I was after, marked them on my map for me before taking me into the museum archive and opening a wooden case, one of a stack of antique boxes containing the archaeological collection of George Holleyman, an RAF policeman posted to Tiree during the Second World War. Seven Stone Age flints sat on a bed of cotton wool. All had apparently come from Balephuil. A label stated:

These flints are almost certainly of Mesolithic age, that is made by the hunter-gatherer groups who populated Scotland before the arrival of the first farmers in the 4th millennium BC. Microlithic (small stone) tools like this were used all over northern and western Europe at this time.

Doc Holliday and I sat and talked more of the Mesolithic.

'You have to imagine Tiree not as it is now,' he explained, 'but covered in woodland; trees stunted, twisted by the winds.'

Pollen analysis had shown the extent of the coverage. I asked which species had been revealed. Doc's eyes stared out before he spoke as though reciting an incantation.

'Alder, birch, hazel, willow, oak, ash, juniper,' he said.

There was abundant fuel, readily available.

'You see, the population would be determined by the worst climate rather than the best,' the Doc explained. 'You have to have enough resources to get through winter.'

The Mesolithic would overwinter on Mull or perhaps on the mainland at Oban, tucked down from the storms and the cold in more settled camps. Then they would adopt a more migratory nature once the spring came round again.

'The entire population of Mesolithic Scotland would only number perhaps five thousand.'

It would be a small collective, perhaps forty or so – an extended group or family – who would head to Tiree in the summer months for flint-knapping. Flint was so vital to the Mesolithic and a seam of flint ran right across the southern tip of Tiree through to Ireland. Doc Holliday traced the extent of the vein of rock with his hand over the map. That was why the Mesolithic came here – for flint.

Nodules of flint would be gathered in places like Balephuil and then worked, knapped. Doc explained the process.

'First, you take the head off, like an egg.'

His left hand swept over an imaginary flint stone.

'Then you work the skin off the flint,' he said, chopping down with the side of his hand. 'Until you are left with the cortex.'

Flint fragments could then be broken off and retouched to refine edges, points and blades. It was skilled, precise work but essential to produce those tools vital for catching, cutting and cleaning food. Stores of flint blades could be built through the summer for the following seasons.

Doc had to go to his meeting. I had to return to Balephuil. We shook hands and said our goodbyes.

So later that morning, I stood on a Mesolithic beach, two hundred yards inland from today's high tideline. It was a perfectly warm summer's day: blue skies and fluffy white clouds. I crawled on a bank of pebbles that ran for twenty yards or so, protected by towering sand dunes ten metres high. I walked barefoot – toe to stone, on all fours, eyes a foot above the ground, peering for flakes of flint. A bumblebee alighted on a golden daisy beside me. I knew immediately – declared out loud that it was a Great yellow bumblebee: a Hebridean rarity.

All day after leaving Doc Holliday, I worked the bank, building a small collection of stone fragments that I laid out on a pad of paper – the larger to the left, smaller to the right, a middle line that might be shell or flint. I smiled at myself, at the ordering, the creation of lines of findings exactly like some Victorian amateur collector. But I had yet to feel the sense that I had truly stepped back into the Mesolithic mind.

I scratched with a broken pencil, scuffing at the surface and pulling out fragments of flint last touched six thousand years ago or so. I pictured a Mesolithic hand holding and dropping. Time had passed. Then my hand had touched and lifted the very same stone splinter from the ground.

It was midday. It was time to leave.

I had been searching the site all morning. It was as I walked away, stepping over the ancient pebble beach, that I saw it.

Grey.

A ghostly grey square of flint sat flat on the surface before me. As soon as I lifted it from that prehistoric beach something shifted. In that moment the cold touch of a past world became tangible – a Stone Age hand touched mine through time. Thousands of years shrank into a second.

It was an arrowhead. An inch or so square, the stone had so obviously been worked away at, carefully retouched to form the sloping edges of the point. The base too had a series of tiny shelves, minute steps where the flint had been delicately chipped away.

That night, as a storm blew in from the north-west, I stared by torchlight at the beauty of that arrowhead. The tent was pitched in the green marram grasses of the dunes, planted between today's beach at Balephuil and the Mesolithic beach of six thousand years ago.

The next morning, I met up with Doc Holliday once more in the museum to show him my finds.

He was wearing the same grey suit. From the car, he carried a heavy-looking doctor's bag from which he retrieved an otoscope. He began his examination, lifting his glasses to the top of his head. His fingers picked one of the smaller fragments I had brought along. He inspected the item.

'Shell,' he said.

I passed the arrowhead over. Under the microscope and lit by a powerful beam, the flint became almost translucent.

The Doc went quiet.

'That's a tanged point,' he said finally.

Over the next week I stepped further back from the

present into the Mesolithic. I walked the coastline of Tiree, scanned the landscape tracing an imaginary line six metres or so above the present tideline where Mesolithic tides would have lapped, then sought out places where people would have sat some thousands of years before to work quietly away at flint. I listened for sounds: for the thin crack of flints being knapped ringing out about the rocky outcrops. Lithic sounds echoed out through time. Click, click, click.

I camped far away from others – out in the machair with the hares, on the edge of the land. I started to learn to shunthe furtive oddity of man. Out in the dunes alone, murmurations of starlings washed over me, startling with their dark shadows, coming out of the summer sun and clouding the skies. I walked prelapsarian lands. A storm blew in and blew out. I crossed to Coll and continued: at night by torchlight scanning the maps, the books for hints of ancient sites, for caves, for places where Mesolithic bodies would have rested. By day, in muddy hollows dotted with hoof marks, I crouched and scratched at the ground. My eyes grew practised at spotting shards of flint in the soil, the sand. Even in the sky, I saw stone. Wandering a hare path one day through the machair at Hugh Bay, a female hen harrier swept over and the pale, flint-white band at the base of her tail stood out clear against her muddy brown coat. In the lee of enormous erratics, I hid from the wind and rain as others had done long before me. Fragments of collected flint chimed in my pockets.

It was during the time I was in Tiree, that I received a letter from the archaeologist Professor Bryony Coles. Some years back, she had single-handedly shifted the scientific community from merely seeing the existence of a prehistoric land bridge between Britain and continental Europe. Instead, Coles had argued, we should recognise a landscape 'as habitable as neighbouring regions' that once existed in what was now the North Sea: a place Coles had named Doggerland.

> If, instead of focussing on land as bridge, we focus on land as a place to be, we may alter ... our perceptions of the North Sea Plain, its significance to contemporary populations, and the implications of its eventual inundation.*

I had emailed her telling of my interest in Doggerland. Her reply told a tale of how she had first become intrigued by the landscapes beneath the North Sea,

---

* B. J. Coles, 'Doggerland: A Speculative Survey', *Proceedings of the Prehistoric Society*, 64, 1998, pp. 45–81 (p. 45).

partly from taking the ferry from Harwich/Felixstowe to Denmark and Sweden, and wondering what lay below ...*

I mused over those words. They framed her own academic obsession; her own wondering. Now Doggerland had become mine, too. I could not stop picking flints from the earth. Fragments of flint littered my world. In the kitchen, a tray presented Doggerland finds. In the study, the Hebridean finds were neatly arranged on show in the wooden compartments of an old medicine drawer. I was becoming an antiquarian.

I read all I could on Doggerland.

Since that first speculative article by Bryony Coles, a great deal of energy and effort had been expended into mapping the palaeo-landscapes of Doggerland. Seismic data from oil and gas industry exploration had gradually revealed the nature of the world lost beneath the North Sea. I read how 'Doggerland was clearly a massive plain dominated by water: rivers, marshes and coastlines.' To Mesolithic peoples, 'Doggerland was a rich environment'. There was fresh water for animals, which meant good hunting; good hunting meant not only food but hides for shelter and clothing; and bone, too, for tools. As the Ice Age became an ancestral

---

* Personal correspondence, letter from Bryony Coles, dated 25 July 2014.

memory, so the climate warmed. Sea levels rose. The creatures of Doggerland changed:

Whilst the colder, earlier period may have seen reindeer and horse hunted, this gave way to deer, pig, bear, wolf, hare, beaver, dog and many other mammals as the area became temperate.

Woodlands flourished. There were fish and shellfish; wildfowl for flesh and eggs. Fruits, nuts and herbs helped to ensure the diet was varied, rich and healthy. For millennia, Doggerland would have been a veritable paradise for generation after generation of Stone Age people who knew intimately the best sites, seasonally shifting over the landscape, and perhaps permanently living on Doggerland.

Yet it would not last. Ice melt meant ever-rising seawaters. Climate change meant marine encroachment; ever more brackish waters meant dying forests. I thought of the skeletal trees sticking from the sands at Ben Acre on the Suffolk coast. I read on.

Doggerland was always doomed … Sometimes slow then terrifyingly fast, the sea inevitably reclaimed ancestral hunting grounds, campsites and landmarks. [*]

---

[*] Gaffney *et al.*, *Europe's Lost World*, pp. 99, 100 & 141.

The parallels to our own age, to our own recognition of climate change in our world, were obvious. I had headed to the farthest edges of our isles to feel the shadow of those past ancestors – in the flint arrowhead I had lifted from that Mesolithic beach; in the shiver as a hare broke from its wild flower cover; as that collective sound of starling wings had swept over me – and yet all along I had shared something else with those Stone Age relations: a foreboding for the future of our worlds.

Bryony Coles noted how in Doggerland as waters rose, so those living there would have adapted their ways:

> For people living along the North Sea shores, the encroachment of the sea will have affected their lives over the generations whether or not it was perceptible in the lifetime of an individual.[*]

I thought of those homes on the North Sea shore today, at Happisburgh and elsewhere, where coastal erosion had wrecked lives. I thought back across eight, nine thousand years to those living in these worlds then.

---

[*] Coles, 'Doggerland', p. 69.

Less than a week on, I headed to Burnham Overy Staithe in Norfolk with Eva and Molly. It was August Bank Holiday weekend. Katie was busy in London but Mum would be there. My sister Helen would be there too, with her family. We would all squeeze happily enough together into the bungalow, our humble holiday home. Each room would be filled with familial bodies – if not there to collect flints and food for the coming winter months, then at least to gather some of the calm goodness which the Norfolk airs could offer and to store them away for darker days.

I had not seen Eva and Molly for a week. They had been away in Spain with their Mum. It was catch-up time. We chatted our way through the winding roads that took us from Essex to Thetford and on, northwards, to the lands of the North Folk.

Uncle John was up in Norfolk too, staying in his caravan for a two-week sailing holiday. He had agreed that one day the following week, when wind and tide were right, he and I would set sail out into the North Sea – beyond the protective arms of Scolt Head Island and the Point – where we would be sailing over Doggerland.

The next morning, we walked in a meandering line of three generations down the dyke. On the wide open sands exposed by the low tide, I told Eva of Doggerland. As I watched her walking the shore, I saw something of Dad in the flow of her arms, some trace of him in her way. I stared and remembered.

When I was Eva's age, Dad would take marathon-long runs over these lands – setting out early over the fields to Holkham and far beyond; running the empty shores, the liminal lands of North Norfolk. He would search for sea urchins along the wrackline on the beach; seek those domed skeletons with their green and purple brushes of colour, their delicate ribbed patterns. He would hold his delicate sea treasures in his hands for miles as he ran. Then he would return from each odyssey sweaty, smiling and out of breath at the bungalow door, handing over his gifts – sea offerings to us his offspring.

I joined Eva on the tideline. There were no sea urchins but a few more brown pieces of ancient peat for our collection: all traces of primordial earth, primeval forests.

'Doggerland!' Eva cried out as she spotted a brown frag-ment on the shore, a compressed remnant of that long-lost world. We gathered together a handful of pieces which broke apart as they dried out in the air – crumbling down, turning back to a rich, peaty soil in our hands.

'Doggerland!' called Eva to the gulls above as she picked another ancient wonder from the sand.

Three days later, I stood by the water's edge. The tide was coming steadily in, creeping up the hard. The wind blew in gusty bursts. I had taken Eva and Molly back to Essex after our Bank Holiday break and then returned to Norfolk. Uncle John stood beside the pillar-box red hull of his catamaran. It had been bought for him by his father back in 1967. Grandpa Canton had been a real sailor, escaping Gravesend as a young lad for a life in the merchant navy. He had taught his youngest son to sail. His eldest son, my Dad, had never learnt. Neither had I.

John's hands worked the rigging, enticing the jib sail into place. He wasn't alone. It was the first day of the regatta. Dinghies crowded the foreshore in various states of dress. Sailors battled with furiously flapping sails.

Uncle John stood out. Whereas other sailors had smart new wet suits and expensive-looking gear, John didn't. He wore denim-blue boating shoes and matching denim-blue shorts. Between them shone a pair of porcelain-white legs. I recognised those legs. They were Grandpa's legs. On his top, John wore a bright-blue anorak secured in place with a banded, orange life jacket. He could have just landed from the 1970s. He looked brilliant.

I watched the mêlée about us. A scattering of Lasers prepared for their race, heading off into the water in drunken, staggering paths. As we prepared to launch the catamaran, a large wooden-hulled boat capsized dramatically just beyond the early-morning crowd of crabbers. Two red life jackets bobbed in the rising seas as four arms reached frantically for their supine boat.

'That's a Sharpie gone over,' someone said.

It was certainly windy; I knew that much. I was trying to keep my head in Mesolithic times even amid the chaos and chatter of sailors preparing their boats. I imagined a collective group preparing to leave a summer camp like south Tiree for the mainland and heard the same sounds of children's voices edged out by older ones calling orders; emotions swilling as they packed the final parcels of goods in the hull. The shifting of the seasons. Time to set sail.

Uncle John was looking strangely at me.

'One of the trailer wheels has a puncture,' he said. 'So if you could push.'

I was millennia away.

'Sure, John,' I said.

I pushed against the varnished hull of the cat, feeling the cold creep as I stepped into the waters of the creek.

'Right,' said John. 'You jump on.'

I did.

Then John joined me, dripping streams of water. And suddenly we were off.

Somehow, he steered a single, straight tack through the flotsam of floundering dinghies down Overy Creek. We raced north. The dyke ran alongside.

'It's like sailing on a dining table,' John had explained the night before in the pub. Now I knew what he meant. The catamaran had no seats, no obvious place to place yourself. Instead, you rather sprawled above the water. It was instantly exhilarating.

In no time, we carved our way into the open waters beyond the marshes, leaving the dyke behind and racing ever faster over the waves. The wind tore in gusts at the sail.

'Keep it tight,' called John over the noise of wind and water. As crew, I was positioned by the mast. I was to keep the jib sail taut. I pulled hard on one rope, battling to secure it in the cleat.

'We should get some speed up now,' John said.

We turned into the wind, heading towards the open channel.

We were flying now. Waves broke against the bow sending showers of cold water into my face. I crouched low. As gusts hit, the right hull heeled, lifting out of the sea and suspended in air for an age before slapping back down again.

In no time, Gun Hill was beside us. Scolt Head Island was on our port side. We shot through the channel, racing along past a vast green buoy marking our way and suddenly we were truly at sea – in the darkening blue waters.

The wind was a south-westerly. We were in the lee of the island, sailing calmly on now out into that bobbing horizon.

The sun had lifted. Lingering clouds had vanished leaving summer blue skies. From my tabletop sprawl I gazed up. The light-mustard of the jib sail splayed against the azure: yellow on blue. I grinned.

We were on a heading for Doggerland.

Later that day, I stood on the sands of the Point at low tide and traced our earlier path in the catamaran. The sun was now setting beyond Scolt Head Island. The green buoy now lay on its side, beached. Wind was lifting the dry, loose sands from the surface of the exposed beaches to form ghostly swirls that whipped about my feet.

I stared out to the sea, thought of Doggerland and imagined the lives of the Mesolithic.

It was a nomadic lifestyle. You migrated from place to place, steering seaways through archipelagos of known islands, kind lands. You followed safe passages first found and forged by persons no longer known, ancestors born many generations ago whose knowledge lived on in the minds of those still walking this world. Learned skills were passed down the line: flint-knapping, sailing, hunting, cutting, curing, cooking. The best sites for fruits, for herbs, for shellfish, for flints were told in tales, in fireside stories for all to remember.

The sun flared white and fell into a bank of cloud on the horizon. As it sank so it lit islands of pale cloud in the sky. The ocean drew gradually back, mysterious and dark, rippling over sandbanks. The sand of the beach shone with that oddly luminescent, golden glow of the low sun vanishing.

In her letter, Bryony Coles had guided me to Margaret Elphinstone's *The Gathering Night,* an imagined account of the lives of an extended family group of Mesolithic folk. The book emphasised how central boats would have been to Mesolithic life. There would have been those epic voyages, sea treks from one seasonal camp to another with streams of boats, generations of families together in their migratory trail. And there would also have been the everyday fishing trips over the dark waters of the lochs or out to sea.

In Doggerland, as the sea rose over the centuries so marine travel became ever more essential. Winds and tides dictated all. In the Early Holocene, the extensive plains of Doggerland extended from present-day Britain right across to the continent. Those lands shrank steadily. Freshwater features grew ever more brackish as marine encroachment turned rivers and lakes to coastlines. Land became sea. Doggerland became a scattered landscape: a shifting coastline, an archipelago of islands off East Anglia, the higher ground of the Dogger Hills still prominent further north.

Yet it may have been one event that changed everything for Doggerland. As Bryony Coles stated, 'single catastrophic events may, literally, have pushed the rising sea over a coastal threshold.'*

One such event was the Storegga Incident.

Sometime around 6000 BC some three hundred square kilometres of rock fell from the side of Norway's coastal shelf into the Atlantic. The vast submarine landslide sent a series of tsunamis out across the eastern coast of Britain. Storm surges following the Storegga collapse would have swept south through the North Sea, straight over Doggerland. Whether this was the moment when Britain truly separated from the rest of Europe remains speculation. Certainly, the event was a catastrophe for those Mesolithic peoples still living around the remaining islands of Doggerland.

In *The Gathering Night*, Margaret Elphinstone painted a powerful picture of the scene as the tsunami hit:

The noise was like thunder far away, only it never ceased. It was not above our heads. It came from under the Sunless Sky. I put down my needle, and stared out to sea ...

The sea was shrinking. The tide was coming in – but the sea was going out. We saw, but also we couldn't see, because it wasn't possible. Out and further out – beyond the lowest tide. Sand we'd never seen before, pale and gleaming. Ripples like stars, and the

---

* Coles, 'Doggerland', p. 67.

frightened crabs scuttling over them. Fish flapping, madly trying to swim in this sudden world that had no water.

'Kemen! The Sea! Look!'

I saw it then, far off under the Sunless Sky. A grey cliff, white-tipped. A cliff made of water. A noise like a mountain falling. My heart turned cold.

And the camp behind us – my mother, my sisters, the children ...

The grey cliff roared like a waterfall. Its sound filled the world. It raced towards us.

We froze.

The grey cliff crashing down. Our world ending

'Kemen, run!'

My body came back to me. We raced back along the beach.

The grey cliff screamed behind us.[*]

In the gloaming light, I thought of those poor Mesolithic souls out there on the islands of Doggerland as the tsunami struck.

The darkness was creeping in. Sand devils whipped about my legs. Flints flickered in the sand. I turned for home.

On the way back down the dyke, I thought too of J. G. Ballard's *The Drowned World*. The book had been published in 1962, the same year that Rachel Carson's *Silent Spring*

---

[*] Margaret Elphinstone, *The Gathering Night* (Edinburgh: Canongate, 2009), p. 56.

announced to the world the true extent of our disastrous stewardship of the earth.

The Drowned World was a strange, dystopic waterscape – an 'insane Eden' – where climate change has flooded the world and where Ballard's anti-hero Kerans travels the tropical waterways by catamaran.[*]

I walked and thought how it is so much simpler to see climate change in vast, dramatic shifts such as the Storegga Incident, in single catastrophic moments rather than the drip, dripping effect of gradual change over centuries – the steady, inordinate rise of carbon dioxide, of sea levels. We were causing climate change. We could still do something to avert the catastrophe. The Mesolithic had done nothing wrong. They had lived for thousands of years in gentle harmony with the earth, gathering what they needed to live and giving thanks for all they took. They had strived to survive causing the least possible harm to the earth.

In the distance, the lights of the village flickered beyond the dark spaces of the marshes. In one hand I felt the soft contours of a piece of petrified wood found on the shore an hour before, yet another fragment from Doggerland, a splinter from those ancient submerged forests still sunk beneath the waves. In the other, I turned a sliver of flint.

---

[*]   J. G. Ballard, *The Drowned World* [1962] (London: The Folio Society, 2013), p. 48.

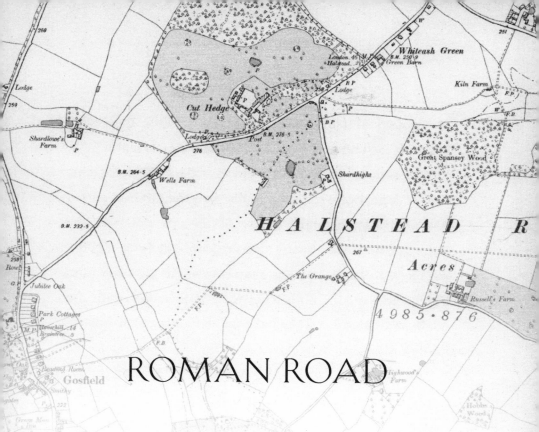

ROMAN ROAD

I carefully unfurled the fraying paper, teasing the folded
sheets open to reveal the full extent of the map. It was so
battered and bruised that the lines of fold had split, leaving a flapping collective of lightly connected rectangles. For
seventeen years, the map had lived in various bags; been
opened in windblown wheat fields and hastily folded up in
rain showers. The map had come to wear its own history
of local exploration – the brown stains of earth and tea; the
circles indicating sites of personal interest that pock-marked
the sheet. The map became not only a general guide to the
villages and surrounds of this square of north Essex, but an

ever reworked palimpsest that altered with the ages, evolving with each new obsessive search of the local lands.

I set about sellotaping the sheets of paper back together. Earlier, a gust of wind had finally torn the tattered map in two. On the kitchen table it now lay like a patient in theatre. I worked with the care of the surgeon, stitching together the ripped edges until the map lay whole once more – a little field-worn in places yet fully functional again and ready to finally face the challenge of finding that missing Roman road.

The Roman road is perfectly straight as all good Roman roads are: a golden line from the white edge of the map through the grey splurge of Braintree town, hiccoughing as it crosses the pale blue, serpentine squiggle of the River Blackwater heading unflinchingly on a north-east bearing with reassuring uniformity as the B1053, before then abruptly changing colour to a dark red shade as it becomes the A1017. A label in black capitals reads ROMAN ROAD. That dead straight red line runs on another couple of miles to the village of Gosfield where it suddenly breaks off at the powder blue wavy line of Bourne Brook, the modern B-road now venturing north in a squiggly, irregular meander. A dark blue biro circle on the map that I had drawn many years back serves to highlight that schism. From that bridging point, the Roman road takes a course unknown for eight miles.

On a line of dead alignment, the Roman road rolls on through the fields of north Essex, a few hundred yards below the pre-Roman settlement at Hill Farm, Gestingthorpe, crossing the Belchamp Brook before stepping across the River Stour and over the county border into Suffolk. Then, just before the antique-shop littered high street of Long Melford, the Roman road appears again – heading straight and true on that same north-easterly orientation as when the road vanishes eight miles earlier at Gosfield.

I had done some initial investigation. The standard work on Britain's Roman roads remained that of Ivan D. Margary, an Oxford don from the 1950s who was a contemporary of J. R. R. Tolkien at Exeter College and whose magisterial two-volumed *Roman Roads in Britain* I had managed to secure from the local library. Margary's textbook offered a comprehensive survey of the entire network of Roman roadways across Britain. He had devised the numbering system that was still employed today to delineate separate Roman roads. The missing Roman road I was after was a section of 33a. It was only when I read Margary's account that I realised the road was no branch line but rather a mainline of the Roman road network. Road 33a ran for some forty-two miles from Chelmsford to Ixworth. It was the southern section of the Peddars Way:

This is the southern portion of the main northern Roman road in east Anglia, known further on as Peddars Way, and it may well have been of equal or even greater importance than the London–Colchester road (3) for it appears to have been planned to give direct access to the coast at the Wash ...[*]

A mile or so from my little cottage there lay not an insignificant Roman road as I had first thought, but one that tore straight through the prehistoric lands of England; an arterial route that ran to the heart of East Anglia where it met an even more ancient roadway that offered a direct route to the Norfolk coast. I thought of the seahenges that had been discovered on the beach at Holme-next-the-Sea – the final destination for the Peddars Way. I thought too of Branodunum – the Roman fort that sat off the salt marshes at Brancaster only a few miles down that North Norfolk coastline. Things were coming together. The Roman road that ran so close beside me – through Lucking Street and Great Maplestead – was only part of the story. It was a link into a far wider appreciation of the prehistoric road network that existed across southern Britain.

The Romans had not simply arrived to find a barren isle; there had already existed a maze of roads and pathways, the

---

[*] Ivan D. Margary, *Roman Roads in Britain* (2 vols) (London: Phoenix House, 1955), vol. I, p. 224.

ancient trackways of the people of Britain. The Romans had built their own road network on top of the infrastructure which already existed. I turned back to Margary and to his 'General Map of Roman Roads in S.E. Britain'. At a glance it could have been a modern road atlas – the hub of London with a spider's web of threads leading away. I followed the solid black line of the 3a from London to Chelmsford, then on to the 33a north until it broke into a series of separated N-dashes: a section labelled as 'course inferred' according to the key (or 'legend' as Margary called it). I turned back to Margary:

> … at Gosfield, the modern road leaves the alignment, which is at first unmarked by any traces beyond the stream crossing, but beyond the grounds of Gosfield Place a straight line of hedgerows and a footmark mark it again for ½ mile to near Whiteash Green, 1 mile to the west of Halstead, and it is possible that the lane direct to the crossing of the River Colne at Doe's Corner may be part of it.
>
> There is now a gap of 8 miles where the course is unknown …[*]

Those were the eight miles of missing Roman road I was after.

---

[*] *Roman Roads in Britain*, vol. I, p. 225.

Then there was that Roman coin. I had found it in the excitement of those first few weeks of moving into the village of Little Maplestead in 2000. A patch of land had been for sale at the same time as the cottage, merely a few muddy yards away over an ancient green lane. The wild open space was too much to resist. We bought it and called it 'The Field'. It was in the days before children. I had bought a metal detector and worked my way from the furthest reaches of the fences until a tiny fragment of Roman Britain had risen from the soil only yards from the edge of the field. The circle of metal was a couple of centimetres across. When it rose from the muddy earth I had shown little initial enthusiasm. A wash and brush revealed a distinct coin. On one side was a profile of a figurehead. The other showed a depiction of a standing stick-like statue with an ornate staff stuck into the ground alongside and what I first took to be a dagger in its scabbard.

When I had next gone to London I had headed for the British Museum and the small hatch in the wall in the coin room where I had handed over my small finding and returned later to receive a two-inch square, white envelope containing my coin. On the cover was written: 'Radiate of the Roman emperor Gallienus (AD 253–68)'.

Now I opened that square white envelope once more. The

coin had recently ventured into my daughter Eva's primary school as their project focus had turned to Roman Britain. The crisp whiteness of the British Museum envelope had vanished. It was fifteen years on. All things fade. Three lime-green crayon lines had appeared. I smiled, heartwarmed. Eva had made a fittingly small protective square out of bubble-wrap to hold the coin. I had sent the treasure into school in another layer, a larger white envelope on which I had written: 'Eva Canton's Dad's Roman Coin'. In pencil, Eva had added: 'Now Eva's'.

I extracted the coin from its various layers and turned its delicate form in my clumsy fingers. The standing stick-like statue on the reverse was actually a genius figure and the dagger in its scabbard was in fact a cornucopia or horn of plenty symbolising abundance and health, an overflowing natural harvest. It surely boded well. I loved how the history of this fragment of Roman life on British soils had evolved a secondary existence since re-emerging from the clay of the field; even if no longer as an object of daily monetary worth, as an object of wonder, a mysterious window into the world that existed on this very ground so long ago. In those fifteen years since it had come to light again, it was as though it had somehow gained renewed life in the air of the modern world some 1,800 years after it had first been born, struck in a distant forge somewhere in Italy.

The idea of seeking the Roman road had been born on a dull day in December. A local amateur archaeologist with a penchant for geophysics had agreed to come out to the field to give it the once over. Tim was a lecturer in electronics. My friend Ellie Mead had put me in contact with him. He arrived one Sunday morning with a car boot full of wooden stakes and measuring lengths. Then there was Aldous. He was from the village. His father was an apiarist – a bee-keeper who placed his hives in borage fields across East Anglia and harvested the sweetest honey. In our tiny hamlet, people rarely met on the street. It was the first I had heard of Aldous, whose enthusiasm for all things archaeological had brought him the mile or so across the fields that Sunday morning.

We made our introductions and I made tea while Tim and Aldous began plotting out the stakes, measuring the rope-edged rectangles which would form the grid for the geophysical survey of the field. I hacked at clumps of brambles that were in the way of the survey while chatting to Aldous of his adventures with Colchester Archaeological Group (CAG).

'Are you going to Wormingford tomorrow? I asked.

He was.

Tim called us back from our chatter. In time the stakes were correctly placed and Tim walked the delineated acre or so of the field with careful deliberation, his delicate electronic equipment peering deep into the earth. The procedure had something of an ancient ceremonial air, as though a practice of sacred divination or a fertility rite: Tim was a wise tribal elder.

The next day was the shortest day. To mark the winter equinox, Ellie had organised a pre-dawn meet in The Crown pub at Wormingford. Those gathered were then to wander down into the wide embrace of the Stour Valley and from there watch the sun rise over the hillside. The river valley site was littered with ancient markings – Neolithic cursuses that now appeared as long lines of gently raised banks in the landscape. A team from CAG had been working on these five-thousand-year-old features for years. Their findings had finally been collected together and now published for the first time. So the Wormingford equinox meet was also a sunrise book launch.

So at dawn the following day I walked the borderlands of Essex–Suffolk with Aldous. We chatted about having an archaeological dig in the village, about seeking out the Roman road. He, too, had spent endless hours plotting the possible course of the road across the local lands; his OS maps also splayed across a desk or kitchen table. The magnetic survey of the field had indicated nothing significant in the area covered. My Roman coin had been found tight to the blackthorn hedge edging the green lane – terrain too tricky for Tim's magnetometer. So there was still hope for finding more Roman material in the field beyond the extent of the geophysical survey.

Though the sun rose through grey cloud, by the time fried breakfasts were being served in the pub, our enthusiasm for the Maplestead Archaeological Dig had been stoked by the walk.

'Lucking Street is the key,' declared Aldous. 'That's where we'll find the Roman road.'

The weeks had passed. There were other things on my mind. In January, baby Joe was born. It was April before I turned back to thoughts of Road 33a. I sent a collective email round to a select band of archaeology friends who might help fashion a more serious search for the Roman road. They were Aldous, Ellie Mead and my old friend Ant who taught archaeology at a local sixth form college. Ant had already said he could get a mini-bus load of students together for a dig. I put a notice in the local Parish Newsletter:

The Maplestead Dig

Join us in the hunt for the Roman Road.

With the help of experienced archaeologists we will be

digging one-metre wide test pits in various gardens of the Maplesteads. We're especially looking for gardens in Lucking Street as there are signs of Roman activity and maybe that's where the Roman road to Gestingthorpe villa ran …

The newsletter editor had added that line about the Gestingthorpe villa. The road actually ran a couple of hundred yards south of the villa but I guessed it wouldn't matter. I didn't want to start getting pedantic.

Within a few days, messages started to mount up on my landline answer phone: a host of local voices offering up their garden to be dug in the fast expanding quest to find the Roman road. One of those that rang had a very local-sounding voice. He was called Jim Lock. He lived over by the ancient woodland of Broaks Wood at Southey Green and he too had been on the trail of the missing Roman road for a number of years. I arranged to pay Jim a visit.

I drove into a sweeping driveway and up to a sprawling bungalow. To the side were a number of cars in various states of roadworthiness. Jim appeared at the doorway along with two small dogs whose yaps extinguished on Jim's command as we reached the vast front room. He directed me to a table where an oh-so-familiar OS map was spread.

'I been looking for that road for years,' said Jim.

His voice held the increasingly rare accent of rural Essex

with its extended diphthongs and yod-droppings like its East Anglian country cousins in Suffolk and Norfolk. Rather than the estuary Essex accent, which had spread from London and now ran wild across the county, Jim's accent was the indigenous one. It reminded me of the old-boy Don who had been my neighbour when I had first begun this quest for the Roman road some seventeen years before. It was the old voice of the countryside round here.

'Were you born near here then, Jim? I asked, even though I already knew the answer.

His long arm unfurled as he pointed through the patio doors to the south.

'Just over the other side of the wood,' he said.

Jim was eighty-three years old. As we turned to the maps, he talked through his own trail after pieces of the past. I smiled as I saw the same pencil line drawn on his map as on mine – from the schism in the straight road from Braintree at Gosfield, marking out the probable path of the road. Jim spoke of the various places he had found Roman pottery fragments in the fields. He rented a medieval barn over by Broaks Wood that he used to store stuff in. We could take a look over there later, if I wanted. I did. Jim said he'd found loads of potsherds simply sticking out of the ditches.

'Later stuff, though,' he said. 'Medieval.'

I lifted a book which was sitting on the table. The cover was faded and worn. I read the title: *The Discovery of Britain:*

A Guide to Archaeology. It was by Jack Lindsay. The name rang a vague bell. The front cover was illustrated with a broken two-handed drinking vessel that had been patched together.

'You know this book, do you?' asked Jim.

Some distant memory flickered but I couldn't trace it.

'No, I don't think so.'

'Well, you need to – it's all about the archaeology of this area.'

I flicked through the pages. Jim wasn't wrong. On the opening page opposite the Contents was a hand-drawn map illustrating the section of landscape from Gosfield to Long Melford with the eight miles of the missing Roman road marked by a string of dashed lines.

'See what you mean,' I said.

Jim smiled.

Rather surprisingly, a young woman suddenly appeared in the front room. She looked like she'd just woken up, even though it was late afternoon. Jim stood up and headed out of the room with the girl, leaving me to Jack Lindsay's *The Discovery of Britain.* I turned back to the hand-drawn map, then to the Note on the page before:

This is a book on Local History – with, I hope, a difference. The stress is throughout on quest and discovery, on the ways in which one gets to grips with the history lying obvious and hidden all round one. The method is often discursive. In such a journey one must keep one's wits about one and be inter-ested in everything. One never knows when some odd detail is going to connect up with another and illuminate a whole sequence.*

Jim returned to the front room, alone but for the two dogs that pitter-pattered among his footsteps.

'Everything all right?' I asked.

'Kids, eh?' Jim smiled.

It turned out that Jim had four children all in their early twenties, all still living at home. The girl was a girlfriend of a son.

'I married late,' he said by way of explanation. 'My wife's twenty years younger 'un me.'

He smiled.

'Oh right,' I said.

I looked at Jim with a new-found admiration. He'd become a dad for the first time in his sixties, and then had four chil-dren. I thought of my baby son Joe who was just four months old. I no longer felt an aged dad. I seemed like a fresh-faced, young father in comparison to Jim who sat before me in his eighties with his brood only just leaving childhood and showing no signs of flying the nest.

---

* Jack Lindsay, *The Discovery of Britain: A Guide to Archaeology* (London: The Merlin Press, 1958), Note, no page.

'Starts with Hill Farm,' Jim said.

He'd turned back to Jack Lindsay's book, to the opening chapter on the excavations at Gestingthorpe.

'Harold Cooper. That's Ashley Cooper's father,' he explained. 'You know Ashley Cooper?'

It wouldn't be the last time someone asked me that question.

'I don't, no. I know of the Roman villa at Gestingthorpe.'

Gestingthorpe was a village close to the dead reckoning alignment of the Roman road. Excavations from the 1950s had revealed a wealth of Roman tiles but evidence too of earlier settlement. I'd walked over the site years back. At some point, I'd head over again. But it was the Roman road I was after.

A week on I walked into Halstead library. A copy of Jack Lindsay's *The Discovery of Britain* was awaiting my arrival. I'd had the robotic woman's electronic message on my answer machine informing me the book was ready for collection but there was no sign of Lindsay's book. It wasn't there. It hadn't arrived due to some computer glitch. Fortunately, my friend Jane Winch was one of the librarians.

'Jack Lindsay?' she said. 'I lent you that ten years ago.'

'Did you?' I said.

'Yeah.'

Jane smiled. I believed her though the remembrance was faint. Now I really needed it again.

'I'm heading home for lunch at one,' she said. 'I can drop it over at yours later today.'

This was library service *de luxe*.

'If I can find it …' she added and laughed.

I looked at the clock. It was quarter to one.

Jane did. That afternoon I lay in the field amid the wild grasses and read Jack Lindsay's book. It really was a remarkable work to find, for the focus was entirely on the archaeology of my patch of Essex. As I started to read, a treasure of local place names fell from the pages. Lindsay began with the work at Hill Farm, Gestingthorpe before turning to Halstead. The book was a fascinating account of Lindsay's work and written in a peculiarly endearing style which incorporated both formal, archaeological jargon and anecdotes on local people and places. Lindsay declared himself 'unofficial prospector and summariser of archaeology for the Halstead district':

You can hope for the pleasure and excitement of new lines of inquiry; but you cannot hope to exploit your finds to any extent. Otherwise you are liable to become a confusing vandal, not a helpful explorer of the past.

It seemed a sensible approach. There were duties to this self-appointed role: 'Your duty is to keep in touch with the nearest responsible centre – here the Castle Museum at

Colchester – report finds and discuss procedures.'

I rolled over on to my back and looked out through the tall meadow grasses to the puffy white clouds that drifted across the sky. A hover fly appeared and droned momentarily over my face. I turned back to Lindsay's words of advice. Suddenly, they read as though written specifically for me.

> So you must enlist as many aids and accomplices as possible ... the prospector must make all use he can of previously recorded work, old newspapers, local histories, churchwardens' accounts, parish registers, and what not; but he must also draw other people in and give them an intelligent interest in what the whole thing is about.

I smiled as I imagined some baton being passed over. I was now unofficial prospector. The Maplestead Archaeological Dig was underway. I felt the hand of history on my shoulder – Jack Lindsay keeping an overseeing eye on my efforts to find that elusive Roman road.

Later that afternoon, after I had read the rest of *The Discovery of Britain*, I headed over towards Lucking Street, walking the green lane at the back of the cottage, thinking about Jack Lindsay and the last sighting in these lands of Margary's Roman road 33a. It was sometime in 1957 as Lindsay was writing *The Discovery of Britain*:

More or less exactly in the dead alignment a flint roadway has been found a few months ago when the front room of the farmhouse on Lucking Street at that point was being refloored.

Lindsay hadn't managed a look at the road before it was covered over once more. He writes how he 'did not hear in time', the frustration obvious. However, he did manage to see a pile of the flints from the metalling, thrown out by the workmen. It was a rare verification of the route, pinning the road to a point on the land, on the map.

By the time that I reached a view of Lucking Street farmhouse, the June sun had warmed. I stood by a stile and halted. I looked down over the stream, the gentle valley beyond and traced the road line that ran without deviation north-east from that front room of the farmhouse, through the newly constructed chicken sheds and the two bare spoil heaps into the open fields beyond. I was due to see the Newtons later – owners of the farmhouse, farmers of the lands all around.

I headed down the slope until I was following the rough line of the Roman road, from a few contour lines lower, along an unkempt footpath, crashing through thigh-high grasses, nettles, sprays of cow parsley. The plaited heads of the corn were just peaking from their green sheaths. The deer came from nowhere. It had been resting and bolted a few yards from my footfall, leaping over the path to the field in one go – all horns and haunch, then powerfully bounding on through the corn to the line of the Roman road where another appeared and the two young fallow males turned back to me and stared before vanishing.

The shock of the deer faded. I gazed up to a roughly drawn line of shrubs that ran parallel, mimicking and perhaps even overgrowing our Roman road. The cornfield met a hedge and became a field of grass – a strip of exposed brown soil prepared for game cover ran up the slope across the line of the road. Halfway up, the land seemed to level out. That was where to seek the Roman road.

I walked on towards the spinney. As I passed the pond, brilliant-blue damselflies flitted by. Two duck-blue billed ruddy ducks sat serene upon the surface of the shallow water. In the still peace of the copse, I sat on the long-fallen trunk of an oak, pulled out the Thermos and settled to stare again at the battered OS map with its green line marking the supposed route of the Roman road. On that dead alignment, the road ran through the centre of the copse, indeed pretty much beneath me. I looked to the floor, the leaf litter. Under these hornbeams, these oaks, these sweet chestnuts and away through this canopy, somewhere very near, the road runs. I poured a cup of tea and turned to Hugh Davies' *Roads in Roman Britain.* Time passed. I read of the techniques used by Roman road designers to map and plot the path; of the

---

* Hugh Davies, *Roads in Roman Britain* (Stroud, Gloucester: Tempus Publishing, 2002).

agger, that raised mound that marks the road; the *metalling*, the materials layer laid to form the solid base; the four layers of Vitruvius from his *De Architectura* – first the *statumen* of stones and flints, then the layers of *rudus*, *nucleus* and finally the *pavimentum*, the paving – supposedly a model for Roman road-building though such layering was way too expensive to find form in reality. That practice wouldn't have applied here, not to a military road through the country, even if it was given the highest importance in Ivan Margary's biblical gazetteer *Roman Roads in Britain* – an 'a': Margary's road 33a. It ran from Chelmsford to Ixworth: forty-two miles long and missing an eight-mile section which ran somewhere beneath my feet.

The average width of the metalling of a Roman road in Britain – the hard layering – was twenty-two *pedes* or Roman feet: some 6.5 metres. The average depth of the metalling came in at twenty inches. I placed my hands twenty inches or so apart and leaned my head to the side as though glancing at the cross section of a Roman road. An oak creaked ominously behind me. I dropped my hands and started to pack up. Surely those figures were a little misleading? Weren't they based on the major roads such as Watling Street or Stane Street, the most important roads, the ones that were still about today? Watling Street had an average depth of metalling, of stone layering, of thirty-two inches. But there was a hoard of smaller roads all across Britain that lay beneath the surface, unseen for hundreds of years. They were nowhere near that width or depth. A horse-drawn carriage had an average wheel base of some five *pedes*, around 1.5 metres, so to allow for two carts to go in opposite directions, the road would need to be some twelve *pedes* wide – a little under twelve feet.

Another week on, the June sun still shone. It was the Maplestead Archaeological Dig week. A dozen students and their teachers arrived at the cottage on Monday morning in a flurry of chatter, mattocks and trowels. I made teas and coffees and we clustered about the kitchen table, which I had laid out in preparation. The battered OS map acted as a tablecloth on top of which I had placed a variety of potsherds from local fields, alongside various articles and books. I gave a short brief as to the focus of the week: to provide some useful digging practice for the archaeology students, and to find that long-lost Roman road.

'The last probable sighting of the road was in 1957,' I stated and sought out Lucking Street farmhouse on the map.

'Here.'

My finger prodded the paper.

Teas downed, we headed out to the field where two first test pits were to be dug, hopefully turning up the hoard from which my radiate of the Roman emperor Gallienus had escaped.

The following day I rescued my bicycle from the shed and cycled over towards Lucking Street. I abandoned the bike by a hawthorn hedge and walked the now familiar footpath. The evening sky offered the hope of rain. The poplars were rustling. Hedgerow birds chattered nervously. A deer came bounding madly towards me through the thick cover of corn. For a moment, I thought it was a wild dog. I froze and stared. It took another bound and then halted and held my stare before turning and leaping back away over the green heads of the corn. There was a strange tension to the evening.

I stepped across the ditch towards the strip of brown soil running up the incline. In lines, young sweetcorn plants were steadily rising towards the sun, the leaves unfurling into their distinctive form. Three hares bolted from their seats, scattering as I stepped on to the soil of the bare field and started to stroll uphill towards that halt in the incline, that levelling that I swore must mark the path of the Roman road. From twenty yards, I could see the three mounds of earth; spoil from the test pits dug earlier that day by the archaeology students.

A lone hare sat further up the field, glancing suspiciously back to me over hunched shoulders. The evening had fallen still. A whitethroat launched its scratchy call from the bush beside the pond. I stood by a hole: Test Pit 1. I leant over and stared at the bottom of the hole. There was a layer of flint all right. But was this really the Roman road? I looked about me. Five hundred yards or so to the south I could make out a single Tudor chimney peering from the tree-line signalling Lucking Street farm, marking that 1957 sighting of the road. I traced the path across the land to here, to this hole beside me. There were a couple of immediate issues that arose. The deep pond at the edge of the field, lined with head-high nettles, was directly in the line of the road. I had assumed the pond marked a spring, that the Roman road might run beside it but perhaps the pond had been built after the road. The second problem was the road itself. I looked down to the exposed layer of flint. It was only a foot or so from the surface, a good twelve inches down but not much more. I wasn't entirely convinced. My eyes lifted. I traced the imagined path of the road, away north through the waves of barley beyond this bare strip of earth and on to the emerald woodland isle of Monks Spinney.

I needed coffee. I walked back down the bare brown soil. I was half convinced, half sure we had found the Roman road. I walked on head down – field walking, stepping over the shrunken sweetcorn plants, seeking signs. Halfway down, in the dry surface soil was an arm of metal, instantly identifiable as half a horseshoe. I scrambled over the ditch on to the footpath back towards Lucking Street where I passed a piebald stallion stood in a field that lifted its head and held my stare, perfectly static as I walked on, and then turned away and returned to grazing.

The culmination of the Maplestead Archaeological Dig was an exhibition of our findings that weekend as part of the village flower show. We had two trestle tables in Great Maplestead village hall that needed arranging so I drove down on the Friday evening with Eva and Molly and a car full of various boxes of finds. Howard Davis, who I had only met thanks to the Parish newsletter piece, had already been invaluable in coordinating the archaeology students as they dug up Joe Newton's game cover field. On the trestle tables were a selection of A4 colour photos of the dig, and a label stating: Maplestead Dig 2015. Howard had printed them off. Eva had created her own Maplestead Archaeological Dig posters. She took charge.

'I think we should put one up here,' she pointed to a spare section of wall.

'Good idea,' I said. 'We can stick the map on the table.'

The following morning we returned to the village hall. As Eva and I fiddled with balls of Blu-tack, Molly played on a set of stage steps. I stuck the OS map to the table. The green line of Margary 33a stood out well. With Eva's posters and Howard's photos there was a good bit of colour to the exhibition. There were also the various collections of findings which Eva carefully arranged. She had created labels for them too. One read: 'My Treasure by Eva Canton', with a red arrow pointing to the various items she had found from one of the test pits in the field. Another read: 'Pond Treasure', and was placed beside a tray containing pieces of clay pipe, small flints and potsherds, bits of chalk and glass that had emerged as we dug the pond last summer. With another blob of Blu-tack, I stuck down the small dark circle of the radiate of the Roman emperor Gallienus that tied the Romans to my field.

We stopped for tea and juice and cake at the newly built marquee in the car park. A battered 4x4 skidded into the driveway. It was Joe Newton, the Lucking Street farmer. I had seen him earlier and he had offered to show me the quern stone he had found years ago when ploughing a field close to Lucking Street. He reached over the rim on the truck and lifted out a circle of grey stone a good foot across. It had a hole in the middle a couple of inches wide.

'There you go,' he said.

It would make a perfect centrepiece for our exhibition.

I arranged with Joe that we would head over to the holes dug by the archaeology students in his game cover field once Ellie Mead got here. She was due around two o'clock with her archaeology friend Jane. I was hoping they would declare the layer of flint a definitive sighting of the missing Roman road.

There was no mobile coverage at all so I pinned a note to the door of the village hall that read:

Attn: Ellie Mead

Meet you here at 2.30!

It worked.

I returned to the village hall with Eva and Molly to find Ellie and Jane quietly working their way around our exhibition. Eva was delighted to have customers and told them tales of her treasures. With Howard and Joe Newton, we headed across the fields in a convoy, parking up by the stench of the vast heap of chicken shed compost, then heading down the lines of young corn as a summer drizzle started to fall.

'Mmm,' said Ellie as we stood over Test Pit 1. 'That does look like something.'

The flint layer, as we had called it, now seemed rather more convincing than it was earlier in the week.

'So the last sighting of the road was at Lucking Street farmhouse in 1957,' I said to Ellie and gestured back to the buildings four hundred yards or so away beyond the chicken sheds.

'If the road runs straight, then this pond here is a problem.'

The steep, nettled banks fell sharply.

'Ah, now I think this is probably a marl pit,' stated Joe. 'Eighteenth century. Perhaps later. But certainly not in the way of the Roman road.'

It was a good shout. Neither Ellie nor Jane could give a definitive word on the road but as evidence we now had a growing collection of Roman-looking potsherds; a possible flint layer of metalling; and, Howard's patterned brass item. It was circular, an inch across and looked like it could have come from a belt or a tunic – a Roman one, perhaps. He had found it with his metal detector right here as the students dug away at the test pits. It was another tantalising piece of the puzzle.

Later that night, when the girls were asleep in bed, I turned back to the Roman road, searching online for information on flint layers in metalling, on *aggers*, on anything that might persuade me further. I was still only half convinced. A dim remembrance of Jack Lindsay's words returned to me:

You can hope for the pleasure and excitement of new lines of inquiry ... Your duty is to keep in touch with the nearest responsible centre – here the Castle Museum at Colchester – report finds and discuss procedures.

I smiled sleepily as I found the quote again. I knew what to do. I hurriedly emailed the Castle Museum:

Dear Sir/Madam,

We have run a local village dig in the Maplesteads nr Halstead (June 2015) in order to seek the Roman road (Margary's 33). We now have a possible flint layer of the metalling exposed and wonder if someone might be able to come out and take a look ...

Then I went to bed too.

The next day there was a reply from Phillip Crummy of Colchester Archaeological Trust asking for photos. I sent them over and soon received a response:

I've never seen metalling like that. Seems far too coarse and not well enough packed I would have thought but could be wrong. There is an edge in the bottom of your pit of course. It looks like the flints are in a cut feature which is filled with flint fragments. It looks more like a foundation rather than a road ...

I had one further battle plan to unfurl. Jim Lock had passed me on to a good friend of his who lived over at Castle Hedingham and who had also spent a good deal of time investigating the Roman road. He was called Colin Peel and was in his eighties, too. He was a dowser.

When I had rung Colin, he was expecting my call.

'Jim told me you'd call,' Colin said.

We talked Roman roads and more specifically of Margary's 33a. We spoke on archaeo-astronomy and then on divination and dowsing. I'd always seen dowsing as a practice of druids and pagans. I was right. It was. Only I was wrong as to what pagans were. The word 'pagan' was derived from the Latin so had in fact been brought to us by none other than the Romans. The Latin root *paganus* merely meant a villager, a rustic or a civilian; someone who was non-militant. A *paganus* was the opposite to a *miles* – a soldier, or one of the army. The word had come from *pagus* meaning a rural district; of the country. So it was a country versus town thing. And it was the Romans who had actually brought the very concept of the town to Britain. So the pagans were actually merely the local British folk of the countryside – as opposed to the townspeople, who were those Britons most willing to adapt to Roman ways. It was not perhaps surprising then that through the centuries the definition of a pagan had gained a rather negative slant, such that a pagan came to mean a heathen as opposed to a Christian or Jewish person; an uncivilised as opposed to a civilised person. By the sixteenth century, the term had morphed even further to mean an illicit or clandestine lover or a prostitute. Yet the term pagan originally just meant someone of the countryside.

Colin told me more of the history of dowsing as a rural practice.

'It was the witchcraft acts of Elizabeth I that really stopped it,' he said.

The terms dowsing and divining were apparently interchangeable though I rather preferred the term divination – it seemed to evoke a magical element to the practice.

We arranged for Colin to visit for a coffee and a chat the following week. He promised to bring his dowsing rods, or divining rods, as you could also call them.

So the following week, Colin sat at my kitchen table. Once we were settled with a coffee and a biscuit I asked him again about dowsing/divining.

'Well you see there's a natural sensitivity that we all have,' he explained.

Colin spoke softly of the process by which he was able to access that natural sensitivity. He had beautiful watery-blue eyes made bluer against the blue collar of his shirt. He wore aviator glasses that hung on a thread around his neck. His grey hair was swept neatly across his head. He spoke of a 'blast of energy' which he could feel when practising natural healing by a laying-on of hands.

'And with dowsing?' I asked.

'Oh, yes,' Colin said and stared with those clear blue eyes into mine.

I had never witnessed the practice of dowsing so we headed out to the field while Colin spoke of Michael and Mary Lines and Dragon and Serpent Lines that criss-crossed the landscape.

'There's so much lost knowledge,' I said. 'I was writing earlier about how there are ways of living and mindsets from prehistoric times that we have completely lost.'

'Yes, yes,' agreed Colin. 'We now live lifestyles that are so much less connected with the land.'

In the field, Colin produced a pair of dowsing or divining rods. They looked like two pieces of wire merely bent a third along their length to form a handle. In fact, that's exactly what they were.

'Fencing wire,' said Colin.

He held one in each hand and we fell into a silence broken only by birdsong. Then he walked forward into the long grass taking pigeon steps while I stood and watched him dowsing. After a few moments, he stopped. The rods were moving. I walked over to join him. As Colin stepped forward over an innocuous patch of the ubiquitous meadow grass, the rods swung in his hands such that the two tips crossed. He stepped back and the rods swung dramatically once more.

'Wow,' I said. 'They're really moving. Is that a normal movement for the rods?'

'Oh, yes,' said Colin.

He looked down to the patch of ground before us.

'I'm never surprised now at the action of the rods.'

He concentrated again.

'Now let me just try to get a fix on the depth,' said Colin.

'Depth?' I said.

The rods seemed to have all the capacity of a metal detector.

'Is it more than three feet deep?' he said.

The rods swung in answer.

'Yes,' he said.

'Is it four foot deep?'

The rods swung again.

'Yes.'

'Is it five foot deep?'

The rods remained still.

'So it's round about a metre deep,' stated Colin. 'Or something like that.'

It was a remarkable introduction to dowsing. I marked the spot in the field with two logs of firewood, leaving them as a cross for digging later.

'That's pretty amazing, Colin,' I said.

He then presented me with the divining rods. I turned them in my hands. They really were just two bent sections of wire.

'I love the fact they are nothing grandly manufactured,' I said. 'In a way, the material is immaterial ...'

'Indeed,' said Colin. 'It comes from you.'

We headed over to Judy and Chris Gosling who lived in Byham Hall, a mile or so away on the northern edge of the village and who farmed a wide tract of land. The predicted route of the Roman road ran right through a section of their land. Colin had visited the Goslings before – on a dowsing trip.

'They're both sensitive to dowsing,' he said. 'You see, it often runs in the family.'

My plan had been for Colin to sweep over those lands with his divining rods and then to whisk him over to Joe Newton's to have a dowse over his lands, too. It was rather ambitious I soon realised. In any case, I discovered Colin had already undertaken his own investigation of the Roman road some years back.

A few days later, I received a copy of Colin's report on seeking the Roman road which had been published in the journal *Archaeology and Dowsing* under the title of 'Minding the Gap: Looking for the 'Missing' Section of Margary's Road number 33 in East Anglia'. It made for fascinating reading. Colin had been guided to hunt for the Roman road by Ashley Cooper of Hill Farm, Gestingthorpe, and had traced the references in Ivan Margary before uncovering further details on the road. A trial dig carried out in 1995 on the Roman road north of Chelmsford found the *agger* merely 3.5 metres wide. Colin had then dowsed along the line of the road to Braintree and on, finding that 'the structural features and dimensions were broadly maintained'. He had followed the road all the way to the River Colne. There the Roman road had vanished. Instead, Colin had divined the road as heading east along the line of the river to Halstead. I read his conclusion:

> My dowsed findings are in line with all the archaeological evidence that has emerged so far, which suggests that Margary was mistaken in his belief that Road 33 followed a continuous unbroken line from Little Waltham, north of Chelmsford, to Brancaster, on the Norfolk coast.[*]

A month on, I was still strolling the fields of the Goslings where I felt that the Roman road ran. I plucked pieces of stone from the surface and in my head saw them as evidence of the foundations of the road. Yet the simple and obvious truth was one I had known for a while. Even if Margary's Roman road 33a did run a few feet beneath mine, it would not be

---

[*] Colin Peel, 'Minding the Gap: Looking for the 'Missing' Section of Margary's Road number 33 in East Anglia', in *Archaeology and Dowsing*, 1, June 2010, pp. 13–14 (p. 14).

revealed as a neat, stone *agger* were I to dig down. All the stone would have been taken centuries ago. It would have been recycled as the walls or rough foundations to the farmhouses and cottages that had once stood, and in a few cases that still stood, all around me. Stone was a precious item in these stone-free Essex landscapes. There had been the best part of two thousand years for locals to pick away at those field findings. Even if the Roman road had ever crossed these lands, its stone foundations would by now be found scattered across a mile-wide ribbon, the length of its existence.

One late summer evening, I met up with Judy and Chris Gosling and we strolled together down the contours, away from Byham Hall. Judy wanted to point out a line of exposed stone in the side of a lake.

'You see we built the lake a few years back,' she explained.

Her young black Labrador puppy bounded beside her.

'Well, the road would have run somewhere close to here,' I said.

I had the battered map in my bag but hardly needed to look at it. By now I knew perfectly well the line of dead reckoning across the landscape. It ran close to the pond in the next field, then ran under our feet and away up the slope towards to the section of wood beyond. Or at least it might do.

Chris pointed towards the western fringe of the wood in the distance.

'See that tree,' he said. 'The one lit up.'

I looked. At an opening in the wood a few yards from its edge was an oak tree whose bark had come away at the base and against which the late afternoon sunlight now struck, lighting up the tree.

'I was once told by the people who owned the hall before us, that there was a Saxon village there,' Chris said. 'Right there by that tree, was where he told me it was.'

I looked again. The tree was glowing in the September sun.

'A Saxon village?' I said.

'Yah,' said Chris.

Saxon was way beyond prehistoric – far too modern to be considered. But it made sense. 'Byham Hall' meant 'the hall beside the village'. Yet there was no village there today. It had simply vanished.

When I turned back towards the hall I saw a man was heading towards us, taking a short cut through the fields. It was Chris's brother Martin. I knew him only from the aeroplane I knew he flew in the local skies above.

'It's a Robin Reliant,' said Chris and laughed.

I didn't get the joke immediately until I realised that Martin's aeroplane wasn't a Cessna but one called a Robin; and as it had three-wheels, his brother called it a Robin Reliant.

Chris introduced me to his brother who had clearly heard the joke before. He shook my hand. I asked Martin if he had ever taken aerial photos of the local lands. He hadn't. Instead, we talked cropmarks – those shadows of sub-surface archaeological features that showed up from the air in freshly sowed fields.

'The best time is when the crops are just starting to grow,' said Martin. 'May or June.'

'And it's the variation in the colour of the crop that you see?' I asked.

'That's it,' said Martin. 'That's what makes them show up. In some fields you can see settlements, roadways, ditches. You can often see them clearly. I'll happily take you up if you want to have a look.'

Some months before, I had vaguely considered trying to use aerial photography to help trace the Roman road but not ever imagined having a local pilot and plane to hand.

'Really?' I said, a little bemused.

'Sure,' Martin said.

He gave me his number.

'Let's leave it until the spring.'

That was fine by me. Perhaps I would get a sighting of that Roman road after all – if not from the land then from the air.

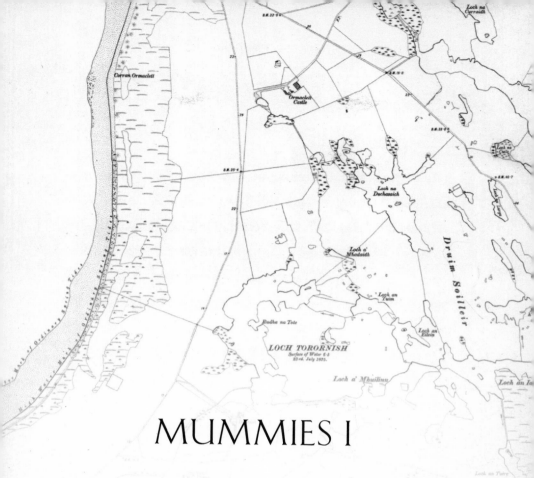

MUMMIES I

I t was earlier that same summer that I first learnt of remarkable findings concerning ancient Britain. Archaeological excavations on the island of South Uist in the Outer Hebrides seemed to suggest a whole new way of looking at the practices of our distant ancestors. A window opened to journey to those faraway lands in August. I would head to the Outer Hebrides to delve once more into the prehistoric past. I would learn from my time on Tiree. Now, I would step back not to the Stone Age but to the Bronze Age.

It was dark and drizzling at Lochboisdale. I stood in a strangely emotional state as I watched these whale-like outlines of islands appearing on the western horizon, rising from the sea as the boat brought me ever closer to these lands. There really was something extraordinary about these islands. I stood on the boat in the damp and the cold of the evening and watched as the sea receded as the land closed in. The boat docked. I was back in the Outer Hebrides.

I drove north to Tobha Beag. A single-track road led through the night, rocky shadows on either side. I turned at the sign for Tobha Mor, passed the ancient chapel and continued along the rough track down to the Howmore River, over the bridge where fresh loch water meets the sea, and there I stopped for the night. A storm was due. It had already flooded southern England and was due to hit South Uist at two in the morning. I slept in the car.

The morning woke grey and overcast. A westerly wind blew gustily. I busied myself, made breakfast and watched the river rushing out to sea as the tea brewed. Two years before, on that very same patch of earth, I had eaten breakfast while watching seven hen harriers – two pale males and five dark females – as they sailed over the loch waters and the wavering heads of the corn in the fields. This morning I saw only one: a lone male. I followed him as he glided the pale sky above the stone bridge then wove out over the dunes to the sea where he vanished into the cloudline.

I passed the next hour on the beach seeking flints and finding none. Tiree still chimed in my mind: the Mesolithic Stone Age, those seasonal summer camps and the sound of flint clink clink clinking on sunny days. Yet that was last summer and eight thousand years ago. Here on South Uist, it wasn't the Stone Age that I was seeking. I was stepping forward in time to the Bronze Age – two thousand years on from those flint-knappers on the beaches of Tiree. Unlike those Mesolithic peoples of last summer, the Bronze Age people I was seeking hadn't travelled for flint, hadn't come journeying, travelling in seasonal migrations, hunting for stone, for salmon, for the resources that would keep them alive in their Oban caves through the bitter winter months. These lands had been their homes. In enclosed, protective roundhouses built of stone and wood, tucked out of the wind and the driving rains, the storms and the cold, they had happily lived out their days here. They weren't seeking stone like those before them. They had forged another way of living – embracing the ways of their Neolithic ancestors in farming the land and keeping animals for food but literally forging too, in a practice utterly unknown to their Stone Age forebears. They were turning stone into metal – to bronze. And they were also doing something here that had only just been realised by the archaeologists who had been digging into these sandy soils for years. They were preserving the bodies of their dead. Over three thousand years ago, the Bronze Age people of South Uist had learnt the ways of keeping their ancestors from rotting away. They had learnt to turn them to mummies.

I walked an untrodden beach and thought about time. It really was a very peculiar item and yet to get anywhere near an understanding of prehistory you had to get a grasp of it, of great handfuls of it really, of what generations of time add up to, what they mean. As I walked, I started to try to reason across the last 10,000 years from the Mesolithic Age to now.

I lifted my eyes from the strandline. Two seagulls passed overhead. The tide was low, leaving a bare stretch of perfectly smooth sand topped with a line of seaweed. The rain still fell softly on my hood.

I tried to think it through. Average each generation at twenty-five years – that makes forty generations in a thousand years; eighty every two thousand years. That's from the birth of Jesus to now – eighty generations. Then go back from Jesus to the early Bronze Age folk of South Uist – eighty generations more. Then step from the Bronze Age folk to the Stone Age flint gatherers of Tiree – eighty more generations of souls who are born, live and die, and then another eighty. So soon, the numbers become mere numbers, not lives. It is so hard to see beyond two, three generations – what of the sight of eight souls, lined up like the descendants of Banquo before me? What then of eighty?

I shrugged the matter away and walked on over sea-sodden sands, out into the open wonder of the beach, peering west to where I had gazed two years ago at the blazing glory of the sun setting over the Atlantic Ocean. Then I turned back to time.

What had changed in all those thousands of years? You walk the same beach through the same seas of stranded seaweed, the same grey swirls of gneiss across the storm beach: the same rocks, the same sea, sky, mountains. What had really changed in, say, four thousand years? The beach looked so clean, so free even from the detritus of our modern world with all its plastic colours. Our world of consumption, of digital entertainment seemed so very distant, so alien, that here on the empty beaches of the Western Isles you could so much more easily step back those thousands of years into the footsteps of ancestors one hundred and sixty generations before. I smelt that salty, so distinct air, of drying, rotting kelp upon the shore. The same sands sunk beneath my feet as had sunk beneath Bronze Age feet. The same sun still shone.

I stopped and scanned the lands for signs of change: a white chapel up on the hillside; a farmer's tractor half-abandoned atop the dunes. Back in the Mesolithic some six, eight, even ten thousand years ago, these lands would have been wooded. Yet the steady work of their distant offspring through the Neolithic, burning and cutting the trees for fuel and shelter and in time clearing land for farming, had ensured that by the time the Bronze Age folk of Uist lived on these lands the woodland had largely gone. Their landscape, their world here on Uist, was beach and then dunes and then machair and then peat moorland up to the stone outcrops of the highest peaks – pretty much as it looked today.

Back at the car I made tea for the Thermos. I was perched behind the car, packing the stove away. When I rose, it was to the sudden sight of a shrunken old lady wrapped in a worn, red winter jacket, the hood pulled tight over her head. I visibly started. In this vast empty place, she had appeared without warning, from nowhere. She stared. She was covered in the same flies that I had been wafting at all morning. She flapped her hands beside her face.

'These flies,' she said.

'They're terrible,' I agreed.

I was still trying to recover from the shock of seeing her.

'Ai. There's a dead gull back there,' she said.

She nudged her head to back along the track.

'Erm,' I stuttered. 'Have they been like this all summer?'

She didn't seem to hear.

'Eh?' she said.

'Have they been like this all year?' I said.

'Eh?' She stared straight into me. 'What's that?'

I repeated myself, only louder.

'No,' she said. 'It's just today.'

She swept her eyes across the skies.

'Something's changed.'

She looked back to me and smiled.

'Got to walk to get away from them,' she said.

'It's better on the beach,' I said.

'Ai,' she agreed.

She turned and went. I watched her walk away then went back to packing up the stove. When I looked again, she was gone. I followed her footsteps some moments later, heading back to the beach south of the river, but never caught another sight of that red jacket.

My feet led me to the open space of the sands. My mind felt as though stunned, struggling to adjust to being here – to the space, to being in these landscapes of endless horizons: sea and sand, sky and air. I gazed about at the grey cloud that was clearing above, and then walked the shore for another hour staring at the tideline for treasure, for ancient stones, signs and wonders. I was in something of a daze. I strolled merrily along, weaving pleasingly through the dunes and fields. Two cars passed. In time, I passed a man in a van speaking into a phone.

'Seven six, seven six,' was all I caught of his conversation as I walked by. And he in turn didn't seem to see me, didn't turn his head as I walked by, as though I really had started to slip, as I had intended, through the structures that hold us in this world. I turned down a sandy path through the machair. A lone male hen harrier flew above the field. I halted, watched that ashen cross glide over the golden heads of corn and shivered at the sight though the sun had started to shine. Then I returned to the car and drove south to Cladh Hallan.

It was twelve miles from Howmore to Cladh Hallan. I reached the dunes in the late afternoon and followed one of the tracks that led into the mile-wide maze of machair. On the western edge of the dunes, I stopped. The sun, though falling, was bright above a bank of cloud on the horizon. By the time I was sat in my chair sipping tea with my bed secure for the night, the sun had dipped below the cloud level for two final hours of splintered daylight before dusk. For the next nine days, I would make a home here. I would seek to step gently into this landscape. I pitched my tent a discreet, respectful distance from the Bronze Age round-houses of ancient Cladh Hallan. Tucked down here, I would start to spend time forging my own understanding of this place, would start to step into this intense, incredible space with horizons that stretched for miles.

I stared west – out into the Atlantic Ocean where the grey swirls of cloud in the far distance were a squall some leagues out to sea that was steadily heading this way. It would soak in seconds, yet would take an hour to reach here even though blown in with huge, hurricane breaths from the Americas. I sat in silence and simply watched the world, glancing every few moments back to the ever-darkening west. To the east, there was a mile and more of soft machair and then a scattering of tiny squares that were the nearest houses. To the north-east, half a mile or so away, sat the stone walls of the cemetery with its smattering of standing headstones; and then, beyond, lay the dark shadowed outline of Beinn Mhor, the highest peak on South Uist. Behind me, to the south, the fertile plains of the machair ran for another mile then turned to marshland, which ran for four further miles to the rocky toes of the southern shore of the island. I drank tea and turned the binoculars back to the north and to the string of three sandy lozenges in the dunes that marked the site of the Bronze Age settlement I had travelled from the further reaches of Britain to visit.

I spent the rest of the daylight reading through my clutch of scientific papers on Cladh Hallan. I sat outside in my dune-top chair until the sun finally fell and dusk was more dark than light. Then I turned in, lying horizontal in my tomb-like tent, reading on by the light Katie had given me for just such moments.

Cladh Hallan was the reason I had come here. It was a Bronze Age settlement, founded around 2000 BC and occupied sporadically until 500 BC. The excavated site consisted of three roundhouses: the north, south and middle houses, though the entire settlement was made up of seven round-houses aligned in a terrace that ran on a north–south axis. In the Bronze Age, South Uist had been home to some two hundred settlements. Each one had been built of stone and wood. Each had been occasionally rebuilt and remodelled, the heavy stone walls lifted and replaced in a similar circu-lar structure a few feet from the foundations of the previous. Each had housed generations of souls.

And those ancient ancestors who lived here at Cladh Hallan lived in a landscape pretty much like that of today: dunes of seashell-white sand and machair grasslands where those roundhouse homes were built; then the moorlands of peat spotted with grey outcrops of stone; and, beyond all else, the peaks of the hilltops that brushed the clouds.

Yet it was the ritual practices that had been taking place at Cladh Hallan which had brought me here. I reread the abstract from one of the scientific papers I had with me:

Ancient Egyptians are thought to have been the only people in the Old World who were practising mummification in the Bronze Age (*c.* 2200–700 BC). But now a remarkable series of finds from a remote Scottish island indicates that Ancient Britons were performing similar, if less elaborate practices of bodily preservation. Evidence of mummification is usually limited to a narrow range of arid or frozen environments which are conducive to soft tissue preservation. Mike Parker Pearson and his team show that a combination of micro-structural, contextual and AMS ^{14}C analysis of bone allows the identification of mummification in more temperate and wetter climates where soft tissues and fabrics do not normally survive. Skeletons from Cladh Hallan on South Uist, Western Isles, Scotland were buried several hundred years after death, and the skeletons provide evidence of post mortem manipulation of body parts. Perhaps these practices were widespread in mainland Britain during the Bronze Age.[*]

The initial excavations at Cladh Hallan had begun in 1995. The article in my hand was published a decade later in 2005 by Mike Parker Pearson and a collective of archaeologists. The title declared: 'Evidence for mummification in Bronze Age Britain'. It was one hell of a statement.

---

[*] Mike Parker Pearson *et al.*, 'Evidence for mummification in Bronze Age Britain', *Antiquity*, 79 (2005), pp. 529–546 (p. 529).

In the northernmost roundhouse, two adult bodies had been discovered. In the middle house, there was the body of a ten- to fourteen-year-old child, probably a girl. And in the southernmost house of the three excavated, there was the body of a three-year-old child. Each burial showed signs of 'mummification and curation of the bodies'.*

And yet that was only part of the tale of Cladh Hallan. The whole story was quite mind-blowing. The findings on the skeletons recovered from Cladh Hallan really had transformed thinking on Bronze Age burial practices. Seven years of further laboratory investigations from 2005 had revealed the true nature of the two adult skeletons. Not only was there evidence of Bronze Age mummification, the adult skeletons at Cladh Hallan really were some kind of Frankenstein's monsters. They had been constructed from the bones of separate individuals. The male adult skeleton, recovered from that northern roundhouse, was composed of the skull and bones of three separate, individual people. The body – the corpus, the torso – was from a man who had died around 1500 BC; the head was from a different man who had died a hundred years later; and the jaw was from yet another man who had also died a hundred years later. A century lay between the death of the head and the body of the skeleton.

---

* Mike Parker Pearson *et al.*, p. 531.

The composite skeleton – a recreated Superman or Franken-stein's monster – had then been buried somewhere between 1440 and 1260 BC. It really was astonishing.

The female skeleton unearthed from that front round-house was also formed of three separate individuals. The body was from a female adult, but the skull was from a male. The right arm belonged to a third individual. It was hard not to label her as some 'Bride of Frankenstein's monster', though perhaps she should rather be seen not as a monster but as a goddess of sorts, constructed from human forms. Her male skull was somewhere between seventy and a hundred years older than that of the female torso – fitted on to that female body and then buried sometime from 1310 to 1130 BC. But the really rather disturbing detail of that female mummy was this: the two upper lateral incisor teeth had been extracted from that male skull and then placed in the bony palm of each hand of the skeleton – the right tooth in the right hand, the left in the left hand.

I shook my head. Though my eyes were tired and my sight smearing, I leafed back through the scientific paper which had first revealed 'Bronze Age mummy is a composite of different skeletons' by 'osteological and isotopic evidence'.*

---

*   Hanna, J., *et al.*, 'Ancient DNA Typing Shows that a Bronze Age Mummy is a Composite of Different Skeletons', *Journal of Archaeological Science*, 39 (2012), pp. 2774–79 (p. 2774).

I laid the wad of papers by my side and closed my eyes. It was too much to take in. Lying in my tent on the dunes, I pictured pale bones tossing and turning in the air, spinning in some *danse macabre*. I'd got the gist of the burials at Cladh Hallan from the accounts I'd read some weeks before. But actually being here a few hundred yards from the site of the burials – miles from any other living being – and having the time to carefully read through the archaeological papers detailing the nature of the skeletons and the specifics of the scientific investigation made real, made visceral, the complexity of the Bronze Age burial practices that had been taking place here three thousand years ago. That was the word: visceral. In all its gory, bloody truth, I could see, or at least I could start to imagine, that solemn ceremony as the cadaver is cut open and eviscerated: the heart, the liver, the vital organs, the viscera, extracted from the body of the dead. I opened my eyes. The head torch forged a patch of light. Outside, I could hear the sea.

My eyes closed again. Raindrops fell, drumming gently on the tent. I pictured the process. Once the viscera had been extracted, the skin and body of the remaining skeleton would have been wrapped, binding the bundle together. Then the skeletons had to be preserved. The outer millimetres of the bones showed evidence of 'unusual thickening of bone mineral crystallites' – a process not due to the alkaline machair sands, but by soaking of the corpses in the acidic peat bog.* The skin and remaining flesh had then been tanned by the bog water. The bones still showed the rusty stains. The wrapped, hollow mummy bundles had been ritually placed in some sacred space, in the dark waters of the peat bog. For weeks, months, the acidic action tanned and preserved the skin and bones. Too long immersed and the bundle would be burnt away. Removed after the right interval of time, the skeleton and its bony parts would keep for centuries.

I opened my eyes again and managed to swat the last remaining fly in the tent with the *Journal of Archaeological Science* article, which left a smear of blood across the phrases 'isotopic evidence' and 'ancient DNA'. Then I turned the torchlight out and the darkness flooded in.

In the morning, I rolled out of the tent to glorious sunshine. I washed, brewed tea and wandered the beach north, already wide awake in this wild new world. I beachcombed the strand-line, then walked down the beach to a spread of rounded

---

* Mike Parker Pearson, 'Cladh Hallan Mummies' in M. Cardin (ed.), *Mummies Around the World: An Encyclopaedia of Mummies in History, Religion and Popular Culture* (Santa Barbara, CA: ABC-Clio, 2015), pp. 67–70.

splinterings of gneiss and turned to treasure hunting, seeking gold coins, Spanish doubloons in the sand. I found none so turned to the stony hard ground of an exposed, ancient beach and sought Stone Age cast-offs. Flint was what I still had in mind – a legacy of Tiree still lingering from last summer; some nice round nodules among all this gneiss beach spree. I found none.

I stopped and stared about me. The simple, sublime nature of all was stunning: the landscape, the seascape, the skyscape. Especially now the morning sunshine had brought out the colour. I passed the incongruous presence of a lime-green oil drum on the tideline, and headed in towards the dunes and the machair and the Bronze Age settlement of Cladh Hallan.

That was when I found the axe. It was the regular pattern of the stone that drew my eyes. I lifted it from the sand and held it in my hand, feeling it fit snugly between my fingers and my thumb. I felt the touch of prehistory. I brushed some stubborn grains of sand from the stone and examined it. It looked like the fossilised bone of some long dead leviathan, the scapula of some strange creature of the sea that had been found one distant day far back in time and then carefully fashioned, chipped at to sharpen that cutting edge. The smoothing action of the sea, the sand and of time had rounded any splintered edges. One of the corners of the blade had come away. Perhaps that was the moment when the stone had last touched human skin – four, five thousand years ago, maybe far more – the moment when the stone was cast off, discarded on the beach.

I held the axe in my hand, motioning a chopping action through the morning air with the six-inch stretch of the blade. I felt the stone against my skin, felt its weight. It had to be a fossilised shoulder blade of some kind. I turned the stone in my hands. One face was a sea of greys; the flip side a spray of rusty oranges. And it was treasure all right – Stone Age treasure. I knew that much.

Yet I also knew that the bedrock of South Uist, as with the rest of the Western Isles, was Lewisian Gneiss, the oldest rock of Britain – from a Pre-Cambrian seam that ran the length of the islands. And Lewisian Gneiss was metamorphic. It was formed under unimaginable temperatures and pressures, deep in the earth and only brought to the surface as molten magma that cooled to leave those black-and-white marbled outcrops which broke the coastline into bays and were so beautiful when washed with seawater. My geology days were distant but I was pretty sure that fossils only really came from sedimentary rocks. I stroked the rusty surface of the stone. Could it be limestone? And if it was, how the hell did it get here?

I needed to move on – to venture forward some five-thousand-odd years from the Palaeolithic into Bronze Age

Cladh Hallan. I tucked the stone axe into a pocket in my rucksack. I walked and thought, threading a path through the machair and the dunes towards the three roundhouses, stepping away from the storm stones and thoughts of flints and gneiss to wondering on bones and Bronze Age burials and to notions of mummification.

I stepped up the slope of the southern dune beneath which the rest of the Bronze Age settlement of Cladh Hallan lay – the four unexcavated roundhouses – then stepped down into the hollow and the three rings of the excavated homes, roughly reconstructed. I sat and stared. Those two adult composite bodies were discovered in the northern roundhouse that apparently acted as some sort of sacred mortuary – a House of the Dead; a Mummy House. Alongside the two bodies there were also the cremated ashes typical of Early Bronze Age burials. A small cremation pyre built of stones lay just outside the walls of that roundhouse. At some moment in time, burial practice at Cladh Hallan had shifted: cremation had been replaced with that intricate, precise procedure of mummification by evisceration and peat preservation. It was a process then followed – anything up to centuries later – by the creation of a constructed skeleton, a united whole of various individuals, to be buried in a ceremony we can only ever imagine.

I shook my head, poured a tea and looked down on the

three circles. I thought of the other burials, the other bodies found during the dig. They were of two children – a ten- to fourteen-year-old who was probably a girl, discovered in the middle roundhouse; and a three-year-old bairn buried some time after death under the southernmost of the three excavated buildings whose body also showed 'post-mortem modification'. I sipped the steaming tea. Were they the children of the families that lived in these houses? Though dearly loved, they had been lost and so were buried within the protective embrace of the stone wall of the family home. Their bones had not been used to form one of those super-human skeletons. They were children; little voices that had grown silent.

I shook my head. The flies had found me. They grew worse, then unbearable. I rose and walked back to the clearer skies of the beach. On the top of the dunes, I found a bright-red drinking bottle with 'USS Gunstone Hall LSD 44 *Defending the Constitution*' printed around a heraldic shield. I stared out to the Atlantic, half expecting to see a warship patrolling the seas. On the beach, the flies were still bad. I flicked at them with the cord of my binoculars then swallowed one, which had me coughing and spluttering, spitting and swearing. There were no spiders to hand so I downed a cup of tea. I sat on the smooth, flat sand by the sea and when I blinked there were more flies – black spectres swarming my vision: *Muscae volitantes.* I blinked again. A strange abstraction seemed to have caught hold of me sat there on that empty expanse of sand. In a while a man walked by, strolling the water's edge a hundred yards from me with a whippet trotting beside him. Something in his mien, his mannerisms, reminded me of my Dad – the hands clasped together behind his back, the head dipped watching the ground as he walked; his worn trousers, shirt and jumper. I watched him as he went by and in time he shrank to the northern horizon and I was alone again on that vast stretch of sands.

In truth I was finding it all rather intense. I spent the night star gazing – praying for an appearance from aurora borealis but instead watching Arcturus sparkling yellow to the west and Capella piercing in the north. As I had risen to turn in, two bright orange-amber eyes had gazed at me from beneath the lip of the dunes five yards away. It was a creature of some kind, though what I could not tell. It held its gaze. Two eyes glowed with fierce intensity like Castor and Pollox. I froze. It froze. For a few seconds, probably just a fraction of one, all else was gone. A midnight stare. Then it was gone. The eyes ducked below, into the darkness. I breathed again, unfroze and headed for the tent.

The next morning, I decided to step away for a moment from those bodies of Cladh Hallan; from the bones, the mummies, the children buried in the floors of their round-house homes. I would venture into an earlier period of the Bronze Age. I would return to Eriskay, a small island to the south, connected to South Uist by a causeway. Two years before, I had seen one of the wild Eriskay ponies silhouetted on a hillside as I had driven through, rushing for the ferry that would carry me to Barra. Today, would be a gentler return; a day of contextualisation. I would look at the burial practices of those who lived on these wild islands *before* the mummifiers of Cladh Hallan. I had a guidebook called *Ancient Uists* which directed me to the cairns of *Am Baile*, 'probably of Early Bronze Age date', which lay on the north-west slopes of Beinn Sciathan. These were the directions:

The cairns are grouped closely together but are ephemeral, and somewhat difficult to find. Take the road from the cause-way towards the Barra ferry. Pass the school on the left hand side, and as the road bends towards the right, walk up the hill, between two streams. The cairns are located on a small level area on the bluff.*

---

* Mike Parker Pearson, Niall Sharples, James Symonds & Heidi Robbins, *Ancient Uists: Exploring the Archaeology of the Outer Hebrides*, ed. Anna Badcock (Comhairle Nan Eilean Siar, 2008), p. 82.

It seemed straightforward enough.

For the next few hours, I pottered about the boggy moorland and the grey rocky outcrops, occasionally spitting flies from my mouth. The sun rose into a gloriously blue sky. I stripped off layers and stumbled on through heather and marshes, weaving every which way between babbling brooks of fresh water until I stopped at last beside a small burial mound of some sort, a smattering of stones that seemed aligned north to south. I sat panting. In truth I felt utterly befuddled. Munching a late lunch, I read carefully through the directions once more while occasionally wafting at flies one-handed. I sat and tried to steady my sense of prehistory, my appreciation of past times. I wondered if it had been the mundanity of my morning that had made me misplace those ephemeral cairns. I had stepped back into the present, had driven in to Lochboisdale to replenish empty water bottles and wash up the pile of dirty pots and pans; then I had gone to the Co-op to load up with supplies – all the time marvelling at the brilliant convenience of modern living. Now, I was perpetually bothered by flies that seemed more annoying than ever. My map flapped awkwardly in the wind. Nothing seemed to flow. I rose, vowed to give up the hunt for Early Bronze Age burial cairns, and instead spent a few moments following the tea-stained waters of the stream nearby, probing the smaller stones with a pencil for Beaker potsherds and seeing pieces of that fine-patterned pottery style in the broken fragments of gneiss littering the water.

I spat another fly from my mouth and admitted defeat. I shook my head and sat down on a stone. What did it matter? The sun shone. The sky was blue. Beside me I noticed the pink, round flower tuber of a marsh orchid, a twin to the one tucked in the lee of a dune beside the roundhouses at Cladh Hallan.

I drove the grey avenue of the stone causeway back to South Uist, then headed west for the standing stone of Poll a' Charra on the southern tip of the island. I parked up and made tea and thought on the tanning process, on preservation by immersion in peat, as I poured the boiling water on to a tea bag in a pan and watched the waters turn to the same reddish-brown as bog water. Just as you leave the tea leaves to do their work, so those ancient Bronze Age bodies were left for that peat water to do its work. It was merely a matter of timing: a few moments for a perfect pot of tea. Too long and the tea is stewed. Leave the bones in the peat water for a few months, and you have a perfectly preserved and tanned mummy. Too long and the acid in the peat starts to eat at the bone tissue.

I walked down to the rocks at the water's edge to drink my tea. It was early evening, the sun dropping, the tide nearly high. I lay with my back against a lichen-encrusted grey

stone and watched the sea. Time passed. There was a flick
of black, of something in the edge of my vision where those
motion-sensitive rods are packed tightest. It was like a fly
– either one of those pesky creatures that had been floating
about my head all day, or one of those more ethereal *Muscae
volitantes* floating across the aqueous humour of my eye.

And then in the globular world of my binoculars, the black
flick becomes a black fin, becomes black fins. Seconds hold
like breath. A black body rises. And another. And another.
And another: four black figures that move together in smooth,
silent motion; slipping slowly through mediums; from water
to air, to patches of sunlight and then back to water.

'Wow,' I say and I watch breathless as they rise again
together.

For endless moments, I follow them as they cross my
horizon, swimming up through the Sound of Barra, feeding
on the fish brought in on the rising tide. They are heading
north, like me. My camera zoom strains on maximum. I click
away until I have a sea of photos of empty sea, and one of the
sleek black body of a Minke whale.

The next morning, I crawled out of the tent expecting more
glorious morning sunlight and found the machair shrouded

in a briny sea mist that closed the horizon to a hundred yards. By the time I was ready to walk north, back to Cladh Hallan, the haze had started to lift in ethereal sheets and as I crossed the dunes towards the roundhouses a cloud of curlew rose too, calling their names as they did so. A chattering of starlings soon followed from a hidden hollow.

At the doorway to the middle roundhouse, I halted respectfully. The entrance faced east and the sun was already high above the sandbanks, the remaining stubborn veils of mists steadily evaporating as the sunlight found the damp, still-sleeping faces of the dunes. The night before, I'd read again the current thinking on the layout of the roundhouse – 'the sun-wise order of roundhouse life'. The living quarters would have been based in the southern section of the roundhouse. Now I stood at the doorway to that Late Bronze Age world, striving to find a way into that world of 1100 BC – into the ways and beliefs of those people who lived here three thousand years back and who practised that elaborate process of evisceration, mummification and peat preservation on their dead. It wouldn't be easy.

I ventured across the portal of the outer doorway, perfectly aligned to the east, stepped into the grassy stone-lined circle where a furnace would have burnt hot enough to cast bronze. It was two strides west, across to the inner doorway, to the roundhouse proper. A hollowed bowl had been carved in a stone that seemed perfect for washing dirty hands and feet before entering the central round of the home. Two huge stones marked the entry point. I stepped inside. Then I halted. I walked to the central point of the roundhouse where the hearth fire would have burned day and night.

I turned east. I tried to picture the rising sun appearing through the entranceway, as new-born sunlight touched the dying embers on the hearth. The fire was relit. The day could begin again. The 'Sun-Wise Model' saw everyday life in Bronze Age Cladh Hallan naturally fitting with the movement of the sun about the earth. An information board explained:

> The movement of the sun around the house gave meaning to the sequence of daily activities and mirrored the life cycle from birth to death, for example, entrances faced the rising sun while burials were in the north-east quadrant. The daily routine moved clockwise with the sun – from cooking to work-ing to sleeping – and is shown by the spread of artefacts found.

I stood in the centre of that Bronze Age room. I turned to ten o'clock, then edged round clockwise to twelve, to midnight, lifting my right arm as I did, as though it was an hour hand. There, the family would sleep together huddled in furs through those long, cold winter nights on a raised 'sleeping platform' of turf banks. I turned through the hours of the night. One o'clock. All lay in deep sleep. One thirty. Two o'clock. The north-east corner, the darkest space in the home, was where the deepest sleep – the sleep of death – took place. It was here the skeleton of that ten- to fourteen-year-old child had been excavated from the foundations of the home; a girl, a daughter. I had read somewhere that she could have been a human sacrifice. I frowned. I thought of my own daughters. How could you sacrifice your own daughter? Or was that the point: an ultimate sacrifice. Or perhaps she had died in childbirth; or just died of natural causes.

I turned clockwise. Three o'clock. Three-thirty. Dawn. Daybreak: the glory of the rising of the sun. The beginning of life again. I faced the entrance in the east. An ethereal spray from the last of the morning's stubborn sea mists swirled about the doorway. I turned in the fresh sunlight of that new-born day to four o'clock. You could almost see those ancient souls awakening to another day and busying with domestic chores: first, stoking the fire and fixing breakfast in the kitchen area; then tidying and brushing the floor. I turned to six o'clock – due south – and on to seven o'clock where the 'working area' lay; to eight o'clock where antler picks and pottery had been unearthed; and then on, round to the west where I gazed up to the now perfectly empty, blue sky.

Back to basics: what do you need to have a stable society that survives; and more, one that flourishes for a thousand years? Or, to be more basic: what do you need to live here on South Uist? First, you need water. Fresh water. Loch water that drains through brooks, streams, rivers into the sea. Like at Howmore just up the coast. That's simple enough. Settle close to a source of clean, fresh, peat-filtered water. And where was the water source at Cladh Hallan? I looked across the three hundred yards of dune to what were called the 'outhouses' – two smaller round houses to the north that were dated to a later era around 500 BC. I'd walked over there yesterday and seen the change in the flora as you stepped into the green horseshoe of what had recently been a sand quarry – those ammophilic, sand-loving grasses like the spiky marrams suddenly vanished and were replaced underfoot with young shoots of ferns and far lusher meadow grass, sure signs of the existence of fresh water coursing close beneath the surface. Three thousand years back a stream had to run close by Cladh Hallan and the string of seven roundhouses. Water. You needed it every day. There had to be a source readily accessible and right to hand.

Water was also central to cultural practice at Cladh Hallan. These people were preserving their ancient ancestors hundreds of years back – generations back. That link to the past, to the ancestors, to the people of the past, was something obviously fundamental to those human souls who lived here three-thousand-odd years ago. And, after the evisceration, after the binding of the skin and bones of the dead, it was immersion in the sacred water that allowed the preservation of those beloved loved ones that came before. It was peat water that allowed their presence to remain in the present. It was the same water that you needed to live.

Bog water. That was where you placed the bodies of the dead once they had been carefully prepared: sacred bog water. In the very same brown, bog water of the peat that babbled and bubbled and gargled its way down from the hallowed high ground in gentle streams; the very same water that found its way down to the low ground where the living lived; and, by some miracle of life, it was the very same water that the living drank and washed and bathed in each day. Up there on the hillsides and the hilltops, rain fell and the water gathered in deep, dark pools and lochs. And from there it streamed down until it ran beside the roundhouse homes at Cladh Hallan where it was fresh and cool and sweet. The very same water: water that kept the living alive and that kept the dead, if not from dying, then at least from disappearing.

I sat down. It was rather too much to take in standing up. I poured another tea. The past suddenly seemed so close;

the ways of those Bronze Age people suddenly felt so touch-ingly human. I looked to the north-east, that alignment to the lands of the dead, to that undiscovered country. I looked to the cloud-shrouded peaks of Airneabhal and Beinn Mhor beyond. Those were surely the places of the dead. The living lived on the low lands; the dead lived on high.

But where did they lay the prepared bodies of the dead? It had to be a sacred place, a place chosen as carrying specific importance on the landscape and a place where a bound body could be carefully left to the preservative powers of the bog water. Not here, not on the coast, on the machair, but on moorland, on higher land where the peat waters were. They had spent ages in an elaborate, precise practice – remov-ing the guts, the vital organs, and then carefully preparing the body for the process of preservation. They were hardly going to then simply toss it into the nearest bit of peat bog and leave it for a few months. The placement of the body into water for preservation would surely have been under-taken with precise care and attention. It would have been a ritual, ceremonial event, one that you could picture as some-thing like that of a present-day funeral – a silent huddle of friends and relatives gathered together as some kind of priest, some shaman, someone chosen by the community who took charge of the ceremony, who directed as the body was prepared and placed into that watery grave not for ever

but for a calculated period of time. I started to see the preservation process as a form of extended baptism for the dead,
a religious ceremony that culminated with the body being
lifted after some weeks or months back to the light of day,
to the fresh airs of Uist from the dark wet world of the bog.

And what of those carefully extracted vital organs
removed from the unmoving body? I closed my eyes and
tried to imagine the scene, tried to peer in, to see those
silent figures dressed in sacred robes as someone under-
took the first incision. Were they putting them into canopic
jars like the ancient Egyptians? I tried to look as the heart
was removed and held in living hands. Where would it be
placed? Would it be burned, cremated ceremonially? Would
the organs be cremated? You can't just have what is, after all,
essentially offal hanging around. Do you feed it to the dogs?
Do you eat it? Do you eat the organs? Would that heart of the
loved lost one be ritually consumed – the remaining blood,
the remaining presence of the dead taken into the bodies of
those still left living, to continue them in you and therefore to
keep them alive? What of the liver? The kidneys? In the same
way that you preserve the bones by that careful bog practice,
why not consume them, or what you can of them, as Catholics
consume the body of Christ each week. Is it so very different?

Then there was that other essential: fire. By the late Bronze
Age most of the trees had been cut down from the islands.

But by that time there was now peat: for fires for the living; and – pulling things together in a tight circle of meaning to life – peat water for the dead. I imagined the smell, that wonderful sweet smell of peat, which would have scented the roundhouses, the smoke seeping from under the eaves; the tremendous aroma of peat that carries so far on the wind and that would have accompanied the daily ways of those people of Cladh Hallan each living moment of the day. I remembered a walk on the west coast of Lewis two years before, heading back to Gearrannan and smelling the smoke from a peat fire burning in one of the blackhouses from a mile away even though the rain fell and the wind howled.

Fire was essential for the hearth. Fire was essential to storytelling, to drawing families together in the darkness. When the day is done and night falls, the bodies can gather and talk, tell stories of the mundane, the everyday and then also of those who came before, keeping them alive not only in the mummification process that kept them physically on earth but in the tales of their deeds, of their time on this earth – all in the warm, peat-scented embrace of the round-house. In the same way that I told tales to Eva and Molly of my father, of their grandfather who had died, the grandfather they had never known, I saw the folk of Cladh Hallan also telling the deeds and ways of ancestors who had died to those who had never met them. Those Bronze Age souls here three thousand years back sat by the fireside and told tales so that the dead remained alive for the living. So, too, I told tales of Dad so that in some way my daughters could get to know him, even beyond death; and so that in a way, in a strange, subtle sense, they could also slowly get to know the parts of themselves that were like him. I, who did know him in life, can see him still in the ways of them. I see him in the gait of Eva as she walks, that long-bodied lean stride with head-bowed over; I see him in Molly's eyes – the same clear-blue, shining light smiling back at me across the generations.

I shook the thought free and stood up. I stretched in the fresh breeze, glanced back to the three circles of stone, then walked away, stepping south over the grassy dune beneath which the remaining, unexcavated, four homes of Cladh Hallan lay. I flicked at the sands of the rabbit burrows with a pencil trying to remember the term archaeologists used for the process whereby ancient findings were brought to light by the actions of creatures like rabbits. I kicked at the odd, pale seashell, then glanced back across the machair, to where my home, my tent, lay hidden half a mile away in the marram grasses. I was getting hungry.

On the walk back I wondered what the past peoples of Cladh Hallan would have done for food. Mainly hunt it seemed. There were no rabbits on Uist in 1000 BC but there were hares and there were lots of deer. I had read that only ten per cent of the Bronze Age diet on South Uist had come from the sea. It seemed odd as they had lived their lives so close to the ocean. But they had turned inland for food instead. They were eating animals. They must have been eating wild, and cultivated, plants, too. I was walking a desire line back to the tent, cutting through the machair, stepping carefully about the yellow heads of buttercups and kidney vetch and rattle; and purple knapweed, white wigged wild carrot and hogweed. Venison and carrot stew threw itself upon my thoughts – bubbling gently away half the day in a pot over the peat fire in the hearth.

When I reached the tent, I dropped down to the sand of the beach and ate some nuts to stave off a growing hunger and then walked south, wandering now, sauntering; worn by the morning, the effort of thinking of the past, my mental weariness gradually eased by the simple act of walking. I stopped after some minutes and took off my boots, then my socks, felt the cool touch of the wet sand on the bare soles of my feet and delighted in the delicate shock. The winds had eased. The sea was calm now. I shaded my eyes and stared to the south-west, out to that ocean of water where the weather came from, out into the vastness of the space above the blue, to the furthest extent of the visible firmament, staring to the infinite distance of the horizon and to the vanishing point where sea becomes sky.

It had been four days and it felt like I was starting to get somewhere. The garments of the twenty-first century had begun to fall away. Not that I was intending to end in deer skins, nor indeed that I felt some deep psychic connection with the Bronze Age humans whose lands these had been three, four, five thousand years back. But rather I was slipping from the ways of now, from the demands of the present, from the mundane and the everyday and somehow getting closer to an understanding of what it was to live here in 1000 BC. And I had already realised that the image of these grim people living out grim lives in their roundhouse hovels which pervaded our collective imaginative vision of Bronze Age Britain was utterly and completely unfair; and indeed quite wrong. That time around three thousand years back was not an era marked by precarious survival. Not at all. Those people were flourishing here in 1000 BC. So often we looked back into the past and saw plague and pestilence and pain. And of course it was a hard life, a really tough existence. The truth was that they lived far shorter lives than ours. But they also lived out their days in a world of peat fires and venison stew. And certainly they lived their lives far more closely connected to the natural world, as one of the creatures of the world that shared this amazing space, this incredible landscape.

I stepped away from the present as I hid out in the furthest reaches of the Outer Hebrides, on the outer limits of land in the British Isles. I learnt to avoid the living. The few lone human figures who I saw out there in those dunes and wild-flower meadows were mainly dog-walkers. I learnt to watch them from afar through binoculars as they wound their way along one of the sandy paths through the machair and to step away if their pathway seemed to be veering too close to mine. I tucked down. It had always been my thinking that if I was get anywhere close to any understanding of Bronze Age existence here then it would only come if I extracted myself from the ways of the present – excepting a few essentials like the Thermos, the tent, the car, the radio at night, books, walking boots etc. etc. I wasn't trying to suddenly live a Bronze Age lifestyle overnight. I wasn't looking to build a roundhouse of my own; to hunt for food and to dress in furs cut from the carcasses of my own kills. But I did believe that I would hardly get anywhere if I was chatting away half the day on my mobile phone to Katie, to Mum, or to friends; or passing the time of day with fellow travellers to these antique lands. That was surely no way to step into the Bronze Age. That was no way to prise open an ancient doorway into the past.

I strolled back to Cladh Hallan, tucking into the hollow of that southern dune that hid the secrets of the remaining four roundhouses of the settlement and disturbing a chattering cloud of starlings that rose and fell again as one, as huge black droplets. And, as I dropped to the dune floor, they were accompanied on their flank by a shade of something, a dark scimitar which rose and cut through the splattering of birds before falling back down to earth. It was a merlin. For an age, I watched as it sat on a fence post, until it flew and was gone for ever.

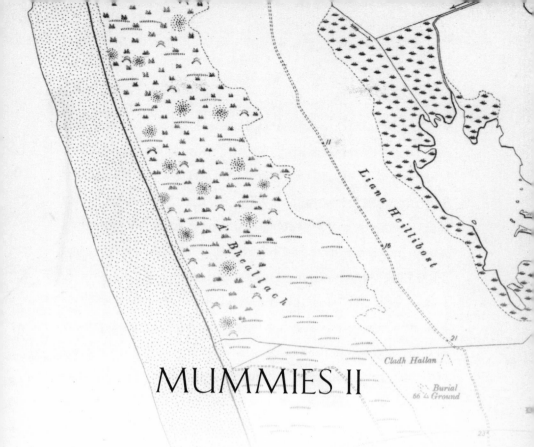

MUMMIES II

A new day dawned. The sun rose slowly through sea frets at Cladh Hallan. I walked north along the sands and then over the green highways of the golf course at Askernish, cutting inland, stepping out of the band of dune and machair which ran beside the sea and into the mile-wide stretch of streams and lochs which would have provided the fresh water for the good folk of Cladh Hallan. I had pencilled in another day of context, of seeking those who came before the Bronze Age mummifiers of Cladh Hallan. I headed for the moorlands, stepping back in time to try to know something of the last of the Stone Age.

Further inland, past the lochlands, I followed sheep and deer tracks through the heather and the marshes and played with the idea of walking back in time. I was heading for Barp Frobost a few miles north of Cladh Hallan on South Uist, and then to Reineabhal, a mile or so further north. I was venturing into the Neolithic – the New Stone Age – on the trail of two chambered burial cairns.

The official dates for the Neolithic ran from 4500 to 2500 BC. Or, to put it another way, I was looking to step back five, six thousand years or so. I was still playing with ways of trying to frame that distance in time. It was so hard to do. First, go back the four hundred years to Shakespeare's time. Imagine yourself in a tavern on the South Bank of the Thames, enjoying an ale in a pewter tankard before you stagger over to The Globe for that new play everyone is talking about – something to do with fairies. Then go back ten times those four hundred years. Or, to try it another way, go back to the birth of Jesus. Imagine yourself in your toga pottering about the sandy streets of Bethlehem. Then go back another two thousand years; and then go back another two thousand years again. That was roughly what the task was. It wasn't easy, this imaginary time travel.

I walked the tarmac of the main road with a smooth, hard stride that took me past a quarry gouging granite from the south face of the hill of Aisgerbheinn. I marched as the road rose, counted footsteps on fingertips until I reached a thousand and then counted a thousand more and reached the rise. I halted at the crossroads. The road to Frobost ran west towards the sea. I remembered my directions were to turn east at this point, to follow the fence line inland to the higher ground. The cairn of Barp Frobost lay on the far side of a stream.

The sun shone. The day grew warmer and the flies grew worse. I crept through a morass of boggy marsh and barbed wire and felt the freedom of stepping beyond as I edged towards the higher ground. I turned my mind to the matter of the Stone Age once more – not to those worlds of clubs and furs and stone axes of the Palaeolithic but to the later, more refined era of the Neolithic. It was certainly still a time of stone tools but significantly now one where cereal crops were grown and animals – cattle, sheep and pigs – were being domesticated for the first time. I walked and thought and sought to imagine, to step into, the South Uist moorland landscape of six thousand years ago.

4500 BC

For thousands upon thousands of years, since the first footsteps, life had been a series of sojourns to favoured camps dictated by seasonal pushes and pulls. In winter, that meant the protection of caves, chosen to be close to fresh water, to be near wood for sacred fire – places that enabled survival through the frozen, bitter months. Eventually, as spring brought increasing daylight, sunshine and warmth, so too it brought a stretching of cramped limbs and the start of tentative steps out and away into the awakening landscape. In summer, there would have been far grander ventures by land and by sea to the further reaches of the known world and sometimes beyond.

And then, sometime around 4500 BC, that shift in living took place.

Hunting and gathering still played a part in sustaining life but now a more stable, more settled sense began to pervade people's relationship with place. The migratory, seasonal aspect to the year, which had so defined the pattern of life for the Mesolithic folk, gradually altered over the centuries as food became available by other means. Certain local patches, favoured lands close to those sites chosen for settlement, now were nurtured with increasing care and attention. Farming became the favoured way of being. Survival no longer meant being reliant on the seasonal resources of everything from flint to fruit to fur. A fundamental change in the relationship between humans, the land and the natural world was taking place.

I looked to the north-east where the grey-piled stone hill of
the cairn was becoming clear against the backdrop of simi-
larly grey rock outcrops. I slowed and tried to picture the
scene here some six thousand years back – in the Neolithic.
They were certainly working stone, and working with it in
new and impressively elegant ways. I had seen a picture of
an amazing carved, black, stone ball that had been found
on Benbecula, a few miles north of Cladh Hallan which had
been carved from granite with such patience, such skill. Since
seeing that image, one of those Neolithic carved stone balls
had become a kind of *ultima Thule* of possible beach findings.

Now I turned my thoughts instead to Neolithic chambered
cairns and the emergence of these huge, new monuments
from the land. There was an obvious, practical sense to gathering these stones when you considered that the task was
undertaken by those prehistoric peoples commonly referred
to as the first farmers. If you were going to farm this earth,
to work this land, then first you had to clear it; and that was
a task that was going to take time – it would take months,
years, even generations of hard labour.

I halted as I finally reached the chambered cairn at Barp
Frobost. Though much of the cairn seemed damaged there
remained an awesome presence to this sacred site, place of

burial, home of the Neolithic dead. I touched an upright kerb stone respectfully, fought to breathe more calmly. Here was the remaining evidence of monumental physical efforts executed in hazy distant realms of the past. I felt the touch of the gneiss, of the lichen; then scanned the horizons. Once, this land would have been covered with trees. Now, there was peat and moor and rock – those long-gone shades of green replaced by browns and greys. The woodland had been cleared since Mesolithic times by hunters using fire both to carve safe spaces for their settlements and to provide grazing for the red deer they loved to hunt. By the end of the Neolithic this landscape looked pretty much like now – minus the fence posts, the telephone wires and the odd abandoned house. Except there would have been those first Neolithic permanent settlements starting to dot the lands of Uist – formed of low stone walls and wooden fencing, enclosed safe spaces defined and delineated from the landscape beyond, where a collective of related souls could sleep in peace together in warmth. They could pen pigs and turn them from wild to domestic creatures, could build a home in a land that would gradually become tamed, too.

I checked the map and the skies, then started off again, heading directly north for the summit of Reineabhal. Over that grey ridge, down the gentle slope which fell towards the still, dark surface of Loch an Ath Ruaidh lay a second chambered cairn, larger and more intact than the one I stood beside. In the warming sunshine, I stepped away – picturing as best I could the process by which this land was first settled, first became a homeland. From those first, palisaded home-steads the Neolithic people of South Uist stepped out and began clearing the land – fathers, sons, mothers, daughters all working together, sweeping the land of grey stone: the largest boulders inched along by gangs of men; the smaller stones collected like eggs by children in reed baskets. Each stone was carried and placed in a defined space, the gathering pile steadily building until in time it would become a sacred place.

There was such a practical necessity to the process of gathering these stones from the land so that the first prim-itive hoes could drill these meagre soils; readying the land for seed, preparing the land in order to eke out a basic cereal crop each growing season from some ancient strain of spelt. This process was a collective practice. It was one that served also to fashion a sense of community, that united the people in a shared goal, firming up their feeling of belonging, both to this landscape, and to those kith and kin who toiled alongside to forge a fruitful way of living here. And, if you as a single individual worked hard enough and were good enough to your family, to your wider, collective kith and kin, then maybe you would be laid to rest in that vast stone chambered cairn, that burial mound that had been created by the communal efforts of centuries, constructed from the stones that were lifted from the earth by those very first farmers and their families.

I reached the summit of Reineabhal and stopped. The sun was now arching over a perfect summer's day. I stripped down a layer and walked over a moon-rock plateau and down the slope into the heather and bog until the pale outline of the chambered cairn became clearly visible in the landscape against the peaty ground. I halted and stared at the site. When I got up close it was the scale of the cairn that silenced me. The stone monument rose five metres from the ground. I walked clockwise around the circular kerb of larger stone tablets that framed the main mound. It was twenty metres in diameter. It was the sheer bloody effort involved that struck home. And this wasn't one of the largest chambered cairns on Uist. What was certain was that this wasn't made over-night. None of these Neolithic burial mounds were. They weren't even made in a generation. They were made over hundreds of years – added to year after year after year.

I sat down and poured a tea. It was so hard to conceive of the collective enterprise that had gone into the construction of the chambered cairn. Nothing in our modern times has such a timeline. Nothing. In the past few hundred years we had learnt to supersede the deeds of the past so swiftly. In Neolithic times, change happened so much more slowly.

I tried to imagine those first figures stepping about these lands, straining to lift, to clear a rough field, and gather the stone on this spot. Here. For year after year. Then I tried to step into that world where the gathered stone became something more – became a place where the dead were buried.

Imagine being here in this land of stone as a young boy. Imagine watching as a beloved grandma is laid out in death and ritually placed in this sacred site. Imagine the silent reverence as those gathered remember, and as the winds tear through the heather, as the rain begins to fall, as the tears fall, as all remember the days of life of that woman whose comforting scent of wool and wood ash you still smell today. You stand as a mite, with five years of life lived, and your tears too are washed by the rain as her still body is carried from the light of day to the darkness of the underground chamber to be placed on the huge granite slab that lines the hallway of the tomb.

I sipped some more tea.

Then you return again, some years later. You have moved away. You are now a man, with a wife and children. You remember the days spent on these lands as a child, screaming at the winds, laughing as you walked the sodden soils picking stones; as a young man lifting ever larger lumps of rock from the land; and now as a man, as a father, here to bury your own father.

It was hard to step into those shoes so distant, yet somehow it felt possible sat on a stone which human hands had lifted and placed exactly here five, six thousand years ago. I leaned against the rock, closed my eyes to the sunlight.

You are tired – that deep-boned tiredness of limbs worn by the labours of life. Twenty-five years of hard living have passed since that day they buried your grandma. A generation ago and now you are here to bury your father whose still face stares up at you. You crouch and creep into the circle of night that is the entrance to the chamber. No tears today. There will be time for such moments later. For now, you must see him away.

And then you return there as an old man. You hope. If the years are good and nothing takes you before then. Time passes. You return to this place and now it is your turn to lie on that slab of stone that marks the halfway between day and night, the hallway beyond the light. The faces of your sons and daughters now stare down at yours.

I returned to the present and to the mewing of a buzzard high beyond. I wondered if everyone would have been buried here. Would it have been only the great and the good that got in, whose bodies found repose in this sacred space? Was it like Westminster Abbey where only the greatest were permitted to lie in the most favoured of locations for the long journey through death's dominion? The mewing persisted. I twisted my head and saw the flecked frame of the bird soaring impossibly high. I pressed my hand to stone. And if this place was one whose gates were locked to all but a select few, then where did the bodies of those others lie? Where did everyone else go? I looked up again to the airs above. I knew the truth was that their bodies were simply laid out to the elements to be gradually devoured by the wild creatures who shared these lands, to be returned to nature.

It was getting intense, this stepping into ancient worlds, into ancient ways and minds. I spent the rest of the day strolling steadily back to the machair of Cladh Hallan, weaving my way west along the track from the chambered cairn at Reineabhal, over the main road and on towards the sea. It was a strange, rather dream-like stroll. I walked past a derelict mobile home which had once been someone's pride and joy but now lay ruined, a side torn away by winter storms, the roof gone. I walked on and passed a grand, abandoned home whose walls and sills stood while the chimney tops leaned drunkenly and grasses grew from the guttering. A line of starlings sat strung along the apex of the roof. I slowed. And then, as I stopped and gazed at this forgotten frame of a home, a white horse walked into what would once have been the back garden, all the time staring fixedly at me. The horse stopped and stood stock still and it peered at me with such intensity of purpose that my skin grew cold under its stare and I turned and walked away down the sandy track to the sea. When I turned back again after some yards, that white horse remained standing quite motionless and still stared intently. And even when I glanced back some distance away, I saw that the horse continued to gaze after me.

I had learnt to hide. I had successfully tucked myself down behind that green curtain of the machair, sliding away from the few figures that walked the tracks nearby with their dogs, slipping down the dunes to the beach and away or merely sinking into the sharp protective embrace of the marram grasses. The sliver of tent lay in a sandy hollow, so low and green as to hardly be seen even by the sharpest of eyes. My beloved car was not so well camouflaged. Its blue hull, seen from Cladh Hallan five hundred yards away, appeared more than once to my glance as an abandoned boat, tossed into the dunes by the storm waves. Yet its presence out there on the edge of the earth, perched on the final scraps of British land before the endless expanses of the Atlantic, seemed to grow ever more natural as the days ticked by. I began to imagine the years passing and the car gently melting into the machair; the blue paint peeling away in time, the tyres collapsing slowly as the rubber lost all solidity, and the rust from that salt air started to take a hold, turning wheel hubs gradually to dust, striping the body of the car to a tarnished skeleton as the corrosive power of this land – this so beautiful, so brutal land – took hold.

The next morning, two cyclists appeared on the track only a few yards away without my spotting them. My retreat from the present and from other people into the ancient world of Uist was rather shattered by the sight of two figures suddenly heading towards me.

'Hello,' a friendly voice called.

I could hardly shun such an affable tone.

'Morning,' I called back.

Andy was a gentle giant of a man. He was perhaps six foot three in height, with a good crop of white hair, and a matching white, stubbly beard. He was wearing a powder-blue T-shirt that flapped about in the gusts of wind.

'I wanted to speak to you …' he started, then paused as his grandson Louis, as I was soon to learn, crashed his bike into a clump of grass.

Andy turned back to me.

'I wanted to ask you about getting my car out here,' he continued.

'Oh, right,' I said.

'You see my daughter is disabled. She has a wheelchair. I wanted to drive her out here …'

'Sure,' I said.

'There's no one out here so she'll be able to get down to the beach by herself. Independent girl, you see. But obviously doesn't want a crowd about.'

'Of course.'

Louis had abandoned his bike for the moment and now stood beside his grandad. His black hair ruffled in the wind. He stared and blinked. His T-shirt simply said the word 'Zoom'. Louis told me he was seven and three-quarters. As his grandad and I started to chat about the wonders of this world about us, Louis disappeared into the land.

They were from rural Lincolnshire, outside Grantham. Andy had an immediately likeable nature. He had been a secondary teacher for years. We chatted about teaching, children, schools and the beauty of this place. I glanced to the south. The building storm cloud still looked far enough away. For a good few minutes more, we stood and chatted together in that glorious sunlight. I was enjoying his friendly company after days alone. Our shared experience of years of teaching forged an immediate bond. His wife, too, was a teacher, a geography teacher. She had served forty years in the classroom. They were both retired now, were here on holiday with their daughter, Louis's Mum, and the vanished Louis.

'I tried driving over there,' he said, pointing back towards the site at Cladh Hallan, 'But there was such a ridge of dunes to cross.'

Andy curved the palm of his left hand to illustrate. He was right. That was the way I had driven over, lurching with surprising momentum over that same dune-bank before crashing back to earth.

'I know,' I said, grimacing as I recalled the noise as my car's underbelly had struck the sandy soils. With a series of finger pointing and squinting in the morning sun, I directed Andy to the more manageable farmer's track, which wove its way here from the southern end of the road to Dalabrog.

'Brilliant,' Andy said.

I glanced back to the south. The storm was due soon. Gale Force 8, the radio had announced of the winds the night before. I had shifted the tent back from the exposed dune edge. It was rather more sheltered now, tucked into a hollow, the roof now only the height of the marram grasses.

Andy had turned to the matter of Louis. We'd been chatting for a while now.

'He loves it here,' laughed Andy as he started to search for his grandson.

I headed over the dunes to the beach. Louis sat in the sand a few yards away with a collection of stones.

'You're Louis, aren't you?' I called through the wind.

He nodded.

I walked over.

'What stones have you got?' I asked.

Louis looked to his blocks of gneiss. Andy appeared over a dune behind us.

'There you are,' he said.

The rain began to fall about twenty minutes later. It was thick, wet rain that soaked in seconds. I had just reached the three roundhouses, dressed in waterproofs that were starting to lose their ability to keep rain out. I pulled a plastic bag from my rucksack and sat down in the lee of the dune, beside the purple glory of that single Hebridean orchid. I was thinking about teeth. I had found a tooth yesterday morning, sitting in the sand kicked up by rabbits in the unexcavated southern section of the roundhouse community. I had turned it in my fingers, holding it by the root as I examined the broken enamel. It didn't look human. I had pronounced it as sheep and popped it in my pocket. Now, I found it there again and extracted it from my damp jacket. I turned it once more in my hand and thought of the 'female' skeleton, found in the front roundhouse. In the left hand of the woman had been placed a left incisor and in the right hand, the right incisor – of a man who had died many years before and whose head in death had been placed on her shoulders.

I shook my head, spinning showers of rainwater from my hood. It was so extraordinary, not just the practices of those ritual burials but the way in which advances in scientific analysis had evolved over the past few years to reveal the details of the mummification at Cladh Hallan. Ten years ago, that same Bronze Age body was viewed as a single female who had been placed in the typical foetal position that so mirrored in burial the earliest womb-warm comfort. Now that gentle image had been replaced with one so much harder to fathom and one that felt in some ways so much darker, too.

Then I retired to the tent, dried off as best as possible, and lay down for a while.

When I awoke, the rain was still drumming on the roof. I stuck to the plan for the rest of the day, which was to head north digging deeper into the prehistoric past of these islands, to drive up to the lochlands of North Uist to another Neolithic chambered cairn – only this one was special. Barpa Langais not only still had its original roofed chamber and inner passage intact, but was described by my *Ancient Uists* guidebook as 'the best preserved chambered cairn in the Outer Hebrides'. The book also noted 'it is possible to enter the chamber (bring a torch), but this is done at your own risk and care must be taken.' I had missed out on a visit two years back on a sunny afternoon passed at the nearby stone circle of Pobull Fhinn. I would certainly take that risk. Now was time to make amends and to further try to fathom that shift in practice, in ways of burying the dead, which occurred from the Neolithic to the Bronze Age.

I drove steadily along the wet road. As I crossed into Benbecula I thought of that black granite ball once more, carved with such dedication by some Neolithic hand. On better days, I would have been eagle-eyed for otters, which occasionally darted across the roads among the maze of lochs and outcrops that make up these southern sections of North Uist. Instead, a murky smirr lingered beyond the windscreen. I concentrated on the road, peering for the turning that would take me away to the north-east.

The rain that had fallen for six hours stopped just as I pulled off the Lochmaddy road. I found myself in a square of tarmacked land which served as a car park for visitors to Barpa Langais. The only other vehicle was large motor home with Dutch number plates parked up in one corner. I stared out through condensation to the misty world beyond. I could just make out the smooth curve of the cairn lying above the land as a false horizon on a rise a few hundred yards to the east. I stepped outside. The wind still blew damp but the rain really had halted, leaving the land looking washed and shiny.

An interpretation board by the track to the cairn was titled 'Early Prehistoric Uist' and illustrated with a colourful vision of brown-clothed Neolithic folk milling about beside the fresh grey walls of the cairn. Three figures were stepping along a raised entrance passage into a stone-roofed chamber. A ceremonial fire was burning. Pale smoke rose past pale stone to a pale sky. I paused a moment, staring at the scene, then stepped beyond the kissing gate and walked the path that rose up the slope east until the cairn became a vast mound of stone before me that shone rain-wet and stretched twenty-five yards and more across. A wooden board planted before the monument read:

NOTICE

Please be advised there has been a recent collapse in the passage leading to the central chamber and the entrance to the chambered tomb has been temporarily blocked in the interests of safety.

North Uist Estate, and a local community group, Access Archaeology, are exploring an appropriate scheme of repairs, which they hope to implement in the near future.

I frowned. The notice ended: 'George H. Macdonald. Factor – North Uist Estate.' Factor: I had come across the word only the day before. It was the name for someone who manages and runs an estate for a landowner. I walked clockwise round the cairn to the entranceway in the east. It was here a hundred years ago that the Victorian archaeologist Erskine Beveridge had dug up burnt bone and potsherds and some flint tools. A wooden frame overlaid with sheep wire was wedged in the opening to the tomb. I stepped closer, feeling the slippery surface of each stone under foot. The wooden frame lifted easily away leaving a black hole against the white lichens and the grey shades of the cairn's stones. The wind blew frantically from the distant sea beyond. I stepped back to that black hole and tucked down into a silent, still world under the protective umbrella of the six-thousand-year-old heap of stone. I looked east along the alignment of the entrance passageway to the chambered cairn, up to the empty horizon of Beinn Langais. Then I turned and crept into the darkness.

The fractured sunlight from the entranceway framed the broken passageway of stone. Torchlight drew shadows from deeper within. A green tint of algae decorated those stones over which the rainwater had leaked and, indeed, over which a dark drizzle now leaked. I crawled steadily forward for some yards through that shadowland, through shades of light and dark until I found myself in the heart of the cairn. A central chamber, roughly pentagonal in form, opened before me. I clambered clumsily into a seated position, my boots bouncing on the stone, my back pack lurching heavily, then leant against one of the five huge door stones that would once have defined this room and, finding a comfortable enough seat, started to stare about me. Each vast slab of stone was a sealed doorway. Behind each was an open passageway into which the Neolithic dead had been placed. My headtorch beam played on the stone. Biotite-rich seams flickered in the artificial light. No sunlight had fallen on these stones for thousands of years. I pictured Erskine Beveridge edging in here a century before and imagined the light of those oil lamps he would have carried into this darkness.

I looked about. Above my head was a six-foot square slab of granite that acted as a central capstone to the corbelled ceiling, a roof piece which dripped dirty rainwater down through a crack that ran much of the length of the flat rock. I peered at that fissure and thought how if that ceiling collapsed now I would be squashed so very flat. Opposite me stood another six-foot square of stone – a door to the passageway that ran away and beyond. By torchlight I traced the five doorways, the five chambers that ran from this central space. Their geometric beauty was remarkable and so impressive considering the sheer scale, the size, the weight of these stone slabs. The creative design so old in conception was still so clear. Barpa Langais had been carefully constructed to a prepared plan. I killed the torchlight and sat in the deep still that flooded the space. Tucked there in the darkness, leaning on that stone doorway, I listened to the sacred silence of that place. The seconds eked away. Once more I tried to think of those ancient people of the past whose heels and footfalls I tracked and followed. Once more I knew that they had not been huddling cold and lonely in this landscape as our age so commonly saw them. They had been flourishing in their prehistoric worlds. I felt the damp seeping through my no-longer-waterproof waterproof jacket, and through the seat of my no-longer-waterproof waterproof trousers. Then I saw those whose elders had laid the foundation stones to this cairn, saw them sat in their water-proof skins, their leather garments gradually steaming dry before peat flames. I saw them fireside in their homes talking in hushed tones of the ceremony they had witnessed – here, at Barpa Langais on the edges of the high land of North Uist.

And then I rose. I had spent time enough in this place of the dead. As my torchlight tore through the darkness once more, I saw the seams of grey ash seeping down through the gaps in the stone, an ancient amalgam of burnt human bone and rainwater working its way through the layers of stone down to earth under the gentle gradient of gravity. To the north-east of the central chamber where I sat, the torchlight lit a broken column of collapsed stone, behind which faint sunlight fell, a pool of half-light exposed where the stone roof of the cairn had recently fallen in. I felt once more the scale and weight of the collective stone about me and started to creep back along the passage which led to the open entranceway away from this other world.

I crawled out into fresh air and billowing winds, then unfurled from all-fours on to two feet and reached up, peering out across the rooftop of the cairn to the west, to where the sun had appeared between layers of cloud, opening pale patches of powder-blue in the sky and lighting darker patches of blue sea in the distance. The wind still blew a gale. I stepped away, along the entranceway towards the east, then ducked back down beneath the protective arc of the cairn and felt the wind fade away. I peered into the damp cracks between the surface stones, seeking shards of pottery, splinters of flint. When none appeared, I sat down against the damp stone and poured a tea, suddenly grateful for the air, the sky and the sun, for the space and light of this world.

For a few moments, I simply took in the scene. I was facing east. On the lip of the horizon, two men appeared striding over the summit of Beinn Langais on the path leading straight for the cairn where I sat. In truth, I was neither prepared for, nor delighted with the thought of returning to the present. But then the notion of that warning notice and my removal of that protective wooden frame returned me to matters immediate. The two men were heading down the hill with evident intent. I glanced to where the frame rested against one of the warning signs, then back to the figures marching my way and wondered if one was none other than George H. Macdonald, Factor for the North Uist Estate. If

I moved now to replace the wooden gate to the entrance-way, my guilt was beyond doubt. I glanced back. Their pace was impressive. As they closed in, I could see that both wore tweed jackets and sported flat cloth caps. Both were six foot tall if not more. My heart sank. It was George H. Macdonald all right, along with one of his henchmen. I rose from my seat on the passageway to the cairn and prepared to mutter some ill-prepared apology.

'Is it open?' the taller figure called out.

The voice that I caught through the buffeting wind rather threw me.

'Erm, yes,' I said with a certain hesitation.

'Excellent,' the voice replied. 'Excellent.'

My eyebrows furrowed. I was standing now, stepping unsteadily on the wet stones away from the open entrance. The two men continued towards the entrance. As our paths crossed, I glanced at their attire of worn tweed and realised they were no Factor and henchman. They had reached the entrance which held an ominous darkness. I saw it at last for what it really was: an ancient black tunnel into a world beyond this, to a sacred land of the dead. The two men had fallen to all fours before it.

'Have you been in?' one asked.

The accent had a certain clipped quality – the bold, brash confidence told of the English Upper Classes.

'Erm, yeah,' I replied.

I started to tell how the wooden protective frame had merely come away from the entrance hole. My stuttering schoolboy explanation was not needed.

'Do you have a torch?' one asked.

'Yes, of course,' I said. 'Do you want to borrow it?'

'That would be very kind.'

I stepped back towards the cairn and handed over the flashlight.

'Wonderful.'

They emerged a few moments later. I could hear their voices echoing in the entrance chamber of the cairn well before they reappeared.

'How would they have shifted all these huge stones?' the second figure was asking me even before he had reached the light of day once more.

'Er, I don't know really,' I mumbled before I realised it wasn't really a question directed at me. 'I, erm ...'

'Rivers and rafts. And using water ...' he replied to his own question. 'It's amazing how many ancient sites are near water. Water's key for moving stone. All the sites on the Nile are on the floodline.'

They walked the pathway east, away from the under-world, as the living had done for eight millennia and more. I placed the wired wooden frame back over the entrance hole before the real Factor arrived. We started to walk back down towards the car park together. The two Englishmen introduced themselves as Barnaby and Bruce. We talked of the ancient sites of the Hebrides. I told them of Cladh Hallan and the mummies.

'On the Syrian coast there's an incredibly ancient site where the bodies were placed under the floor of the living,' said Bruce.

'Ugarit?' I asked.

'Yes, that's right. Ugarit,' said Bruce. 'They had the bodies under the main living space.'

It was close to twenty years since I had been at Ugarit yet now the thought of that site instantly brought back a remembrance of a six-foot long grey snake that had lifted from the grey stones before me. I felt the shadow of a cold shiver.

Bruce was a little taller than Barnaby, a little more dapper too with a neat neckerchief and a rather less torn tweed jacket. His knowledge of ancient sites of the world was soon evident. Barnaby knew the Outer Hebrides sites with an affection built over many years.

'There's a sense in which the stones feel like ancestors,' he said at one point in our conversation.

I asked if he lived here. He didn't but had been coming to the islands every year since his first visit when a student at St Andrews.

'Gets into your blood, doesn't it?' Barnaby said. 'Really bites in.'

He told how each year he rented the same house for a fortnight, inviting different friends over to share time and adventures together.

'Friends have nearly drowned ... boats overturned,' he said, clearly only half in jest.

'It is such an amazing place here, isn't it,' I said. 'Every day is just so intense.'

We reached the car park. I asked if they had seen the slightest sliver of the new moon the night before, as it had risen through a miasma of mauves and maroons at sunset. They hadn't.

'I'm afraid the whisky sours had rather taken over by then,' said Barnaby in comic confession.

We said our goodbyes and went our separate ways. I watched the outlines of Bruce and Barnaby strolling off down the road in the dusk, then climbed into the car, slipping out of the wind to a sudden silence as the door closed. I needed a moment. I simply sat for a while watching the open plains of the coast beyond the windscreen then stepped back out into the embrace of the wind, turning back to the pale arc of Barpa Langais on the hillside.

From there, five hundred yards and more away, the cairn lay symmetrical on the landscape. It was hardly believable that it had been built by human hands. I stood and stared then turned back to the present. Before me, on the edge of the car park, was a dark, raised mound of peat turfs, a stack of drying sods, or, in Gaelic, a *cruach mhònach*, as I later learnt. The symmetry with the stone stack of the cairn on the hillside behind was hard to ignore. A wooden paling stuck out from the turf stack. I leant forward to read what was written in black felt-tip:

H P
A E
R R
R K
Y I
   N
   S

1

H

7 hours

→

I looked about as the light thickened, wondering. I smelt the smoke of that Donegal peat my old friend John Burke had presented me with a year back – handing over two black blocks of turf from the stash in the boot of his car. The peat before me was still fresh. It would need time drying. I pondered the morality of English appropriation of Scottish peat. A bagful. Ten turfs. Would Harry Perkins mind? I wondered. I thought of Seamus Heaney's grandfather 'nicking and slicing neatly', as the turf was cut from the earth.* I saw the spade as it struck down into those sacred soils. In the end, I took a golden coin from my pocket, which gleamed in the evening light, and placed it carefully on a turf. Then I covered it with another. And then I took ten turfs, lifting them with due ceremony, tucking them into a bag, then into the boot of the car before muttering words of thanks to Harry Perkins.

Then I drove south along the empty road to my dune home.

Another morning broke. Light flared across the dunes. Wind tore through the grasses. Tomorrow I would be waking for the last time on these sandy soils. Tomorrow a boat was due to arrive soon after dawn which would take me back across the Hebridean Sea from South Uist to the mainland isle of our archipelago. I had one final day at Cladh Hallan.

---

* Seamus Heaney, 'Digging' in *Death of a Naturalist* (London: Faber, 1966), p. 14.

The night before I had once more read through the pile of
archaeological papers on Cladh Hallan and had turned my
thoughts back to Bronze Age life here around 1100 BC. I had
lain in my tent as the wind and the rain played about outside
and heard in horror at midnight the news from the BBC
World Service of the beheading of the eighty-one-year-old
archaeologist Khalid al Assad at Palmyra, Syria. I had shuddered, actually shuddered, at the news, my body quivering
for a second, and sparking the remembrance of a morning
many years before when I had risen from my hotel bed well
before dawn and stepped outside into the dusty streets of
that same antique city of Palmyra and had walked about,
past the stone remnants of a shattered civilisation, the colos-
sal wrecks of temples which had once been proudly raised
from desert sands and that lined the modern streets. Last
night, I had seen again the same snapshot I had witnessed in
the dusky pre-dawn light of that distant morning – a simple,
horse-drawn, wooden cart that rattled along the street beside
me; and I had seen again that glimpse, that glance, as the
jalabiya-clad Bedouin driver had flicked his reins and turned
his shrouded head to me, as he had looked at me in that
half-light of dawn, the only other soul about that morning.
Something in that man's way, something in his mannerisms
and his actions, as he had turned, had made me think of my
father who had died not a year before. At the time, I had felt

an odd sense of helplessness, of utter incomprehension, as I had been drawn by some unfathomable thread to the remembrance of my father by that lone figure on a deserted street in Palmyra. It had seemed in some strange way, as I stood in the stone remnants of that ancient civilisation, as though we two were the last human beings in this world. There, in the street before dawn, I had stopped and had watched the horse-drawn cart and its driver as they had trotted off down the road and had heard the waning echoes of the horse's hooves as they had faded into the distance, until he was gone and I alone remained in that antique land. And then I too had turned and had walked away, silently stepping from the road to the sand beneath the fallen pillars, the skeletal remains of a temple in whose empty embrace I had cried, shedding tears that fell like raindrops into the dry desert.

I shook the night thoughts from my head and turned to the day. I was due to meet Kate MacDonald, a South Uist-based archaeologist, at the roundhouses at eleven. Over breakfast I reviewed the building list of questions I had for Kate, then spent the morning scanning the wrackline, dreaming now of finding one of those carved, Neolithic stone balls of which some 425 had been found to date; largely across the length of the Scottish mainland and islands with a few examples in Northern England and Ireland. These petrospheres, as they were properly called, dated from the late Neolithic to early Bronze Age. But the fact that really intrigued was that the vast majority were almost exactly the same size – around seventy millimetres in diameter; roughly the size of an orange. Each ball was carved by Stone Age hands from a dark igneous rock at least three thousand years ago and decorated with a variety of ornamentations.

So I scanned the smatterings of rock litter as I sauntered north along the beach towards the golf course at Askernish, stepping once more up through marram grasses and away from the sand to the dune tops and the smooth green slope of a fairway. I was on the tenth tee. I lay back on the soft green grass and stared to the grey skies, listening to oyster-catchers calling from below. Some days back when walking this way I had plucked a golf ball from the machair rough. A few of those Neolithic carved stone balls had been found with exactly that same dimpled, golf-ball style of ornamentation. On the beach that day I had then found three small buoys, each a few inches in diameter and each, too, with that distinctive dimpled pattern. Though I wondered as I lay on the tee, the wind whistling above me, if perhaps these round findings – the golf ball, the collective flotsam of buoys – were some form of a sign, I searched the shoreline in vain for a prehistoric stone ball.

Back at the roundhouses, I waited for Kate MacDonald until she appeared around the dunes – a diminutive woman with distinctive, dreadlocked hair and a nose ring. Kate was followed by a black Labrador who lumbered up to me in introduction. Her dog's name was Holly. Kate had kindly agreed to pop over from Lochboisdale on a lunch break from her consultancy work with Uist Archaeology.

We stood by the circle of the northernmost roundhouse. I offered Kate some coffee. We talked dogs at first. Kate joked how she and Holly were often poking their heads in rabbit holes: Kate for signs of ancient bones and potsherds; Holly for signs of rabbits. I said how dog-walkers were the only people I'd really seen out here.

'It made me realise they would have had dogs,' I said. 'You get warmth from dogs; you get protection, you get friendship. Just as we do now.'

'There were two buried in one of the houses,' said Kate.

'Of course,' I said turning to the site before us. 'They were sacrificed, weren't they?

'Yeah,' said Kate. 'The fact they were sacrificed suggests they were really important rather than the other way round.'

'Wasn't there a thought that the ten- to fourteen-year-old girl might also have been sacrificed?' I said remembering last night's rereading.

'Yeah,' said Kate. 'It's possible. It's hard to tell. The only ones that are definite sacrifices are the dogs. But of course, it's quite easy to kill someone without leaving a trace on the bones.'

'Of course,' I said.

'They do some things that seem very bizarre like that. It seems odd to us because we're looking back into a society that's very different, that's happy to have bodies buried in the floor. There are things that we do now that will seem really odd in the future. Someone was talking to me about brochs the other day, saying how they were pretty useless. But think of football stadiums. They're not there for any practical purpose but we still build them.'

'And football stadiums won't be around in four thousand years,' I said. 'But brochs still are.'

'Yeah,' said Kate. 'And there are loads of little cultural things that we do – like laying out cutlery in a certain way. Little rituals. In a way, they define our society.'

The coffee had already gone cold. We wandered to the middle roundhouse where that ten- to fourteen-year-old had been buried, along with those two sacrificed dogs. I wanted to hear Kate's thoughts on life out here three thousand years back.

'I was thinking about how they were flourishing, weren't they,' I said a little over enthusiastically.

It was a word I had started to use rather often to describe Bronze Age life on South Uist.

'The thing here is that you have a really good buffer against starvation,' said Kate. 'If your crops fail or if your animals all die, you can get down on the shore and pick winkles and cockles.'

'Though only ten per cent of their diet was sea food,' I added.

'Yeah, but it's that security,' said Kate. 'And that applied here until quite recently, to be honest. Many people here still don't understand why you'd pay good money for shellfish. It's seen as poverty food.'

The wind had picked up. Kate's lunch break was being stretched. But I wanted to check with her one other point that seemed to be coming clearer to me.

'Is it right that there were some two hundred settlements along the South Uist machair in the Bronze Age?'

'Yeah,' said Kate. 'It would have been busy around here.'

'I mean I've been trying to do the stats,' I said. 'I reckon that means some two thousand people living here: men, women and children. That's about what there are here now, isn't it?'

'Yeah,' Kate agreed. 'I reckon so.'

We were right. I checked later and the latest census showed a figure of 1,754 for the population of South Uist, which had actually fallen by sixty-four in the decade since the last survey. Roughly that same number of souls had been living here three thousand years back.

A horrible crunching sound was coming from a few yards away on the sandy path. Kate and I looked over. It was

Holly. She was munching the bones of a dead rabbit that I had seen earlier in the day. It had been eviscerated: probably by a Golden Eagle.

'Holly,' Kate called through the wind.

She headed over to pull Holly away.

Our time was up. Kate had a heap of paperwork to wade through back in Lochboisdale. We said our goodbyes and I went and sat beside that lone purple orchid. When I rose a few moments later the figures of Kate and Holly were still walking the dune path away to the north. I stood a while and watched them until they stepped over the hillside and were gone.

That final night a gale blew. At dusk, I stood in the howling wind on the exposed hilltop of Beinn a' Charra. Beside me stood a five-metre-high standing stone.

When I got back to my home in the dunes and sat by the edge of the world a while, the sea spat salty drizzle into my face, driven by the storm winds. The essential point that I had realised in my short time here was that those Bronze Age communities of South Uist before could comfortably deal with this landscape, even with these extremes of weather. They were indeed *flourishing* here. The word kept ringing in my mind. Those folk of the Bronze Age had forged homes and settlements and lifestyles that had really worked; that had enabled them to keep warm, well fed, and comfortable. They had forged ways of living that allowed them to cope and survive and yet so much more – to live lives well lived. The Bronze Age people of South Uist had developed delicate ways of being, touches of culture that we could only faintly understand today, which indeed the finest minds of our modern archaeologists, scientists and thinkers were only vaguely starting to get an inkling of. They had lived close to the landscape that surrounded them, close to the natural world which they relied on and yet had built into their cultural existence ways of memorialising their loved ones that made our funereal and burial practices seem almost crass and uncaring in comparison.

Of course it had been hard. They were living in a hard world. As Kate MacDonald had said earlier today with perfect understatement, the winters here were tough. They always had been. They still were. The dark and the cold and the driving storm systems that whirled and whipped across the Atlantic and struck these low-lying Hebridean Islands with such brutal natural violence did so in prehistoric times too. And South Uist took the brunt of it all. Yet what the first findings of the work here at Cladh Hallan had undoubtedly started to show was that there existed another side to life here three thousand years back, and especially in the ways in which the lost loved ones were treated by the community, both in their death and burial and in the manner in which they were preserved in the hearts and memories of those who lived on after.

To live on the land.

That was the great division between those Stone Age flint seekers of the Mesolithic who I had been chasing last summer on Tiree and their offspring who would become the Neolithic. It was the Neolithic who had really been the first ones to turn places like this from landscapes to be seasonally enjoyed, to be travelled to in order to gather the foods and materials that would allow survival through those ridiculously tough winters. The Neolithic had forged homes here. Rather than fleeing as the seasons turned – as the sun fell and the days turned darker – the Neolithic had stayed out here on these exposed islands. They had remained. They had forged settlements. They had lifted those first stones to form the first rough fields to drill and sow with wild seed. They had started to turn sites of wilderness into homelands. They had captured and tamed wild animals to form livestock. Those Neolithic folk had become the first farmers in Britain. They had driven stakes into the land and settled and made homes. That was the vital change. That was what had shifted everything, for in doing so they had effectively turned and seen the darkening skies, and had known the severity of the test of winter which they had to survive and had trusted in their ability to do so.

Before those first Neolithic proto-farmers and settlers, life had been seasonal and migratory. I had seen fragments of evidence of that nomadic lifestyle on Tiree – that tanged-point flint arrowhead; the scattering of microliths I had lifted from the beach; the stone detritus of the summer camps cast aside eight, nine, ten thousand years before in solidly Stone Age times. Those lives had been itinerant – travelling the seasons, setting up camp rather than settling the land. There was such a clear contrast to those first farmers of the Neolithic or the metalworkers of the Bronze Age. Those Stone Age people were living lives of movement dictated by the seasons. They would stir and rise and migrate once more as the darkness of the winter months died and the days lightened. They would return in kin groups to travel the lands to favoured sites: where the salmon ran, where the flints lay plentiful on the fresh storm-lines of stone dredged from the ocean floor on to the beaches of distant islands far across the seas.

You would travel first as a child and be taught to read the landscapes, the routes to the summer camps. You would travel in extended family bands, and meet other kin – on the flint beaches, round firesides, while gathering, while hunting. And all the time you would learn the ways to survive.

But first you would have to find your way both to the migratory landscapes and then once there, to the places of plenty. There would be mental maps of migratory pathways passed down through the ages. Those early peoples of the Stone Age had to leave signs and markers to mark the seasonal pathways through the landscape. They had to make secure the knowledge of those vital migratory routes both through the maze of seaways and islands, and on land through the labyrinths of dunes and moors and hills and mountaintops. They would have used the natural landscape to find their way but they also raised vast stones as markers to help to guide the way, and in so doing were securing signs for all future generations of kin who would later seek those seasonal pathways. And as they raised those stone markers so too they must have felt a feeling of security, of embedding themselves into the very landscape itself. Surely that was the truth of standing stones. I thought of Pol a' Charra on the southern tip of South Uist where I had sat and watched those minke whales some days before. Then I thought of the towering monument of Beinn a Charra I had just returned from, not an hour before, whose presence was visible for miles – even in the gloaming light of dusk.

Standing stones were raised as significant sightlines, as markers for Stone Age travellers on the land and seas. Those future Neolithic generations who followed would do more to manipulate the landscape than raise huge stones to mark the ways. They would lift the stones from the land to form the first fields. And with those stones and rocks they would form burial sites which would eventually become the grand, chambered cairns like those at Barpa Langais. And once such palaces of the dead were formed, where lost loved ones were kept to be remembered and memorialised, the hold to that place, to that landscape, would soon become forged not across lifetimes but across generations.

Once you as a people have moved beyond a mode of survival to a way of living that allows you to complete the tasks that you need to complete to survive then the basic essence of life has been successfully secured and something more than mere existence can emerge. If you as an extended family can complete that process of living year in and year out without injury, infection and illness, without being exhausted or going mad or being killed by someone else; without freezing, without starving ... then you can start to create ways of thinking about the world. More time can be turned to thoughts on the world, to thoughts on the meaning of life, the meaning of death.

'Where has our mother, our father, our grandfather, our grandmother, even – God forbid – our child, gone? Where have they gone? And what do we now do with the body that lies still here?'

Those questions need answers. How they are answered forms part of the survival package. As a collective of people you need to get some form of ritualised way of dealing with death or else you don't survive. That aspect of living – of dealing with the death of loved ones – is one each society must deal with or it will not endure. And here at Cladh Hallan three thousand years ago, the ways in which they were fulfilling that task – with mummification, with preservation by a ritual intricacy way beyond that of our own society – surely tells us something of the complexity of their world and something too of the incredible manner in which they were flourishing on these edges of the British Isles.

I turned my head south to the steering point of the incoming squall. Seawater sprayed my face. I licked my lips and smiled at the taste of salt. I was snug and warm in my layers of clothing. My waterproofs were worn but would at least keep me dry against this smirr. It was August after all. I would turn in soon. For the moment, I was savouring these last few hours of my final night on Uist. There was still some lukewarm tea to be had. I poured a cup and stared out into the darkening storm.

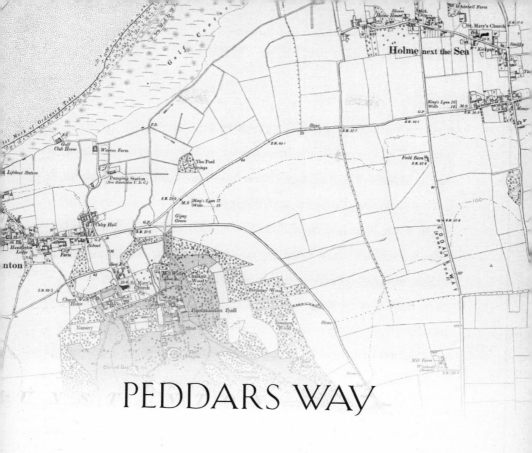

PEDDARS WAY

S oon after I returned from South Uist I began planning. For a good while I had been wondering about a walk along one of the ancient roadways of prehistoric Britain. Since seeking that lost Roman road through my homelands in the heat of the summer months, the impetus had grown ever stronger.

For this adventure, an accomplice was needed – a friend who would happily walk for miles in silence but who would talk when those miles began to drag. I knew Paul would be perfect. Our friendship had been forged beside fire pits and in pubs over pints across fifteen years or so. He lived two villages over in Alphamstone. He'd been brought up in rural Wales, the eldest of three boys. He had been a surfer, a dry-stone waller and a philosophy student. I'd met him soon after moving from London to the fields of Essex and life experiences had brought us close. I knew that though I might struggle, Paul would have no problems with walking fifty miles in two days. He did triathlons. He worked as a gardener, keeping a small rural estate perpetually in glorious natural beauty. Last year, he'd done the forty-odd-mile Lyke Wake walk across the North Yorkshire moors in a day.

In The King's Head one night, I asked if he fancied walking the Peddars Way.

'Yeah,' he said. 'Definitely.'

The only matter to sort was juggling our family commitments so I popped round one weekday night. His wife, Amanda, arrived back from a late night at the school where she taught. Paul and I had been getting overexcited over a glass of red, looking at possible dates. There was a window at the end of September.

'Sure,' agreed Amanda. 'That works.'

Suddenly, we were sorted. We'd both drive to Burnham Overy Staithe on the North Norfolk coast. We would stay in the bungalow on the Saturday night, and then take one car to Thetford the next morning. After that, it was simply a case of stepping into two pairs of prehistoric boots and strolling the Peddars Way through the Norfolk countryside. We would pitch tents around Castle Acre on the Sunday night and get a good meal and a few pints in a pub. Then we would head off again on Monday morning and arrive at Holme on the Norfolk coast that evening to see the site of the early Bronze Age wooden wonder of Seahenge – though the oak henge itself had been removed for preservation. Then it was either walk the extra ten miles or so along the coast to Burnham Overy Staithe or camp in Holme the night and complete those miles the next morning.

'We could catch the bus,' I said with a smile.

I knew that the reality of the extra ten miles along the Norfolk coast might not be that appealing.

'Or get a taxi,' Paul suggested.

Either way, by Tuesday afternoon, we'd be back in Essex – me to collect Eva and Molly from school and Paul in time for his son Marley's parent consultation. Perfect.

September grew more glorious as the days shortened. On the lanes and footpaths, dog walkers happily stopped to chat in the sunshine. Talk was of an Indian summer. I spent the time inside. The task of unearthing the history of the Peddars

Way was proving rather more involved than I'd imagined. Essentially, the Peddars Way as a walkable path today ran from Knettishall Heath in Suffolk for some forty-six and a half miles to Holme-next-the-Sea on the North Norfolk coast. Most agreed that rather than a prehistoric road it was probably Roman in origin. A glance at the arrow-like precision of much of the route running on a NNW to SSE axis made you instinctively agree. Yet the far more ancient chalk ridge route of the Icknield Way, which ran for some two hundred miles from south-west England, led precisely to the starting point of the Peddars Way.

I had borrowed from the library three Ordnance Survey maps that covered the route of the Peddars Way and unfurled them with inelegant haste in the kitchen. I found Thetford, and then Knettishall Heath four miles to the east where a large white letter P in a pale blue square box marked the seemingly far too convenient point where the prehistoric Icknield Way transformed into the Roman Peddars Way.

I had read somewhere that the Stone Age travellers who followed the Icknield Way could well have followed a path that ran *west* of the Peddars Way, winding via the flint mines at Grimes Graves a few miles from Thetford and then on north along the raised chalk ridge to the sea at Holme. On the map that now covered the kitchen table I followed the high ground marked in the form of serpentine orange contour lines. I traced the parallel swirls of forty-five- and fifty-metre markers, spotting the tiny '45' and '50' orange numbers as they appeared just above Ickburgh, scattered here and there like tumuli markers. I followed them to the northern edge of the map and then, with further inelegant unfurling, tracked them north on to the next map – the chalk ridge running a roughly parallel path to the straight line of the Roman Peddars Way.

Here was a perfect illustration of the variance between prehistoric and Roman roadways. One wound a path along the contours of the landscape. The other tore through the land. Both might take a route roughly from A to B – Knettishall Heath to Holme in this case – and yet each told of a very different relationship to the ground they travelled over. The chalk-ridge route of that northern arm of the Icknield Way meandered gently through the sandy Brecklands towards the coast just as Edward Thomas had declared that 'the earliest roads wandered like rivers through the land'.* The Roman Peddars Way told quite another tale – even in the manner in which it was constructed as a hard *agger* upon these soft soils. The road was a route to be marched along. It was suddenly so brutally clear, so obvious. The Peddars Way was a military road just as Margary's 33a was. And what

---

* Edward Thomas, *The Icknield Way* (London: Constable, 1916), p. 1.

I suddenly realised in my utter blindness to the absolutely obvious was that it ran directly through the centre of Iceni tribal lands. These were Iceni territories that the Peddars Way ripped through.

It might well have been the case that an earlier, pre-Roman route had run close to the Peddars Way. That road could well have been part of the Icknield Way and so also part of The Great Ridgeway which ran through Neolithic southern Britain to the tin- and gold-mining lands of Cornwall way off in the south-west. So the earlier route was part of that network of prehistoric roads that criss-crossed Britain. Yet the Peddars Way, as visible today, was part of that rigid pattern of lines that had been etched across the British lands by the Romans. I turned back to my photocopied pages of Ivan Margary's *Roman Roads in Britain*. On the map labelled as 'The East Anglian Network' a mesh of fragmentary bold black lines illustrated the pattern of Roman roads, both those whose course was 'certain' and those whose course was 'inferred'. The Great Road 3a ran from London to Chelmsford where it forked – the 3b thrust on towards Colchester, the 33a struck north to Braintree and boldly on before splintering to a fractured line of dashes. That was the missing Roman Road I had spent the summer searching for. I knew well that hiatus, that lacuna on the landscape of Roman Britain, knew those white spaces between the dashes as sods of earth walked and rewalked, as holes in corners of fields dug down to where the hard *agger* of 33a should be. The road reappeared in bold black again as a stubby line below Long Melford, then more confidently headed north-east, on past Ixworth. At Coney Weston, Margary had another fork – the 33b – which after striking north to Roudham Heath, edged west and ran arrow-straight to the Norfolk coast. It was labelled in neat, quaint and capitalised copperplate letters: PEDDARS WAY. So the Peddars Way which Paul and I were due to walk was actually an extension of the Roman road I had spent much of the summer seeking.

Sunday morning was sunny. All seemed auspicious as we reached Knettishall Heath and a leaf-litter strewn car park. It was the perfect day for a walk. A party of walkers were crossing the wooden stile nearby. Fingerposts pointed to north and south. To the south: Icknield Way–Ivinghoe Beacon 105 miles (169 km). To the north: Peddars Way–Holme-next-the-Sea 46 miles (74 km). The sign seemed to be stating that it was on this very spot that the prehistoric pathway of the Icknield Way actually transformed into the Peddars Way. I puzzled at the sign a second more and then noticed the symbols on each wooden marker: the Icknield Way fingerpost had a round, white circle like a perfect full moon; the Peddars Way had a stylised pale acorn against a black background. I frowned and returned to matters in hand. I laced up my walking boots and lifted the rucksack to my back.

I felt the load on my shoulders.

'Not *too* bad,' I thought.

We each had a tent, sleeping bag, minimal change of clothes, snacks and water. We'd divided the other essentials. I had a Thermos of tea. Paul had his well-worn Trangia stove and some meths for fuel. I had somehow already managed to misplace the National Trail Guidebook to the Peddars Way I'd got from the library which had neat sections of Ordnance Survey maps to guide our way. My thinking had been that it saved bringing the three OS Explorer maps needed to cover the route of the walk and avoided the faff of unfurling them. Now we had none.

'We don't really need a map, anyway,' I said. 'It's a straight line to Holme.'

We just needed to walk. And that was what we did – stepping enthusiastically over the stile on to the soft ground of the beech woodland at a brave, bold pace. We had already been chatting confidently – cockily even – on the speed we would walk.

'Four miles an hour is certainly doable,' I'd reckoned the night before. 'And, for some sections, maybe five.'

My back-of-a-fag-packet calculations told that at an average of four mph we would only need to walk for six hours each day to cover the forty-six-odd miles to Holme. That meant if we pushed it for the first couple of hours we could pretty much stroll the rest of the day.

We struck out through Blackwater Carr and soon were stepping via the footbridge over the Little Ouse whose waters formed the county border between Suffolk and Norfolk. The path wove into a tree-lined avenue.

'Spindle,' Paul said rather suddenly.

He reached a hand out and, without halting or breaking stride, neatly took one of the bright pink pods that were hanging from the shrubs all around us.

'Eh?' I called back.

The path had forced us to walk Indian file.

'These are spindle shrubs,' Paul said.

'Oh, right,' I said.

They were certainly quite a startling sight, drooping with lurid pink colour.

'Erm … *Euonymus europaeus*, I think,' he added.

'Impressive,' I said.

They were everywhere, on each side of the pathway and shrouding our route with a ridiculous pink vibrancy. I pulled at one of the pods without dropping my pace. It fell to the floor. On the third attempt, I caught one in my hand

and examined it as I marched on. The pod was a centimetre across and made up of four segments. It was that gorgeously rich, rosy colour that amazed. I stared closer.

When I glanced back to the spindle bushes they looked as though they were bearing some surreal offering of fluorescent popcorn – hanging freshly cooked and ready for passing wayfarers to munch on. They even looked oven warm.

'Can you eat them?' I asked.

Paul laughed.

'Not sure,' he said. 'And as we've got forty-odd miles still to go, perhaps best not.'

'True,' I agreed.

He offered a handful of sweets instead: toffees in pale gold wrappers and brown-striped humbugs. I took a humbug – Paul passing the sweet rather like a baton in a relay, both of us shaving a tad off our pace and then stepping up again once the handover was safely complete.

We were having a ball. The sun was still shining. The forecast was good for tomorrow, too. It was the end of September but camping out was going to be fine. No rain, no cold to contend with. The ground was dry and sandy. The path opened up and we sped along, crossing the River Thet and then on, the path steering dead straight and true now apparently on a setting for the magnetic north.

Two miles on, we passed another ancient roadway, the Harling Drove or the Great Fen Road, which wove off west through the sandy Breckland soils and eventually away to the even flatter, black soils of the fenlands. Drovers may have driven their animals along that track for hundreds of years, but for thousands more it had been one of that prehistoric network of paths connecting together significant sites of ancient Britain. We walked on north over Roudham Heath. I had read some time back that this common land had been the gathering place of the Iceni, the legendary Celtic tribe of southern Britain who, under the leadership of Boudicca, had risen up against the Roman presence on these isles. If it was true then it was here that those Iron Age warriors gathered back in AD 60 before they headed south to burn the Roman *colonia* of Colchester to the ground. I found the reference some days later. Even if not from a primary source, it was still intriguing:

It has been suggested that Boudicca's call to arms was met here on Roudham Heath. This was the place where they started their march to Colchester by heading, presumably along a path that became the Peddars Way, to Knettishall and on to Coney Weston.[*]

---

[*] Ray Quinlan, *The Greater Ridgeway: A Walk Along the Ancient Route from Lyme Regis to Hunstanton* (Milnthorpe, Cumbria: Cicerone, 2003), pp. 227–8.

Boudicca had led the Britons on, massacring much of the Roman Ninth Legion sent in to relieve Colchester, before heading south with ever increasing numbers of British rebels to burn down both the Roman cities of London and Verulamium (St Albans). Though the Romans had been on the ground for nearly twenty years, Roman rule over ancient Britain was only truly established after the death of Boudicca. The re-securing of Roman control over these lands by the Roman Emperor Gaius Suetonius Paulinus after the Boudiccan Uprising meant a banishing of the old pagan ways that had prevailed for so long. The battle that took place in AD 61 probably somewhere in the West Midlands, perhaps close to the Roman road of Watling Street, had been fought between the pagan forces of the past and the soldiers of the new militarism which Roman invasion had brought. And that battle, fought in the heart of England, was for the dominance of a way of living: either the old ways of the Britons, or the new-fangled materialism of Rome. Rome won. The death of Boudicca ended a way of existing in the landscapes of this archipelago that traced an ancestry back to the earliest Stone Age.

We struck on. Our way was dead straight – not the gentle, contoured route of an ancient path through the land. On we went, marching along as seemed so fitting with the increasing signs of military activity in the area. We had ventured into the eastern edge of a vast section of the Norfolk landscape that had been sectioned off for military training in 1942. Some 30,000 acres had been requisitioned. It had been a huge enterprise, undertaken to ensure the creation of a secret military training zone tucked away in the middle of Norfolk. One thousand people had been evicted from their homes.* Villages and hamlets such as West Tofts, Stanford, Sturston and Tottington were abandoned. They still are. Their churches remain but no parishioners live within their parishes. And even today the area is used by the military for live firing exercises, for mass parachute drops and large-scale battle enactments. Paul and I marched on oblivious. Birdsong rather than bullets filled the air. Perhaps it was one of the few days each year when the military put down their weapons. We sucked on humbugs and chatted happily away.

At the village sign for East Wretham, we halted a moment to take a photo of the roadside that simply read 'Peddars Way'. That was the moment I discovered my smart new camera wasn't working.

'It might be the batteries,' Paul suggested reassuringly.

---

* Bruce Robinson, *Peddars Way and Norfolk Coastal Path* (London: Aurum Press in association with Natural England, 2009), p. 34.

'Might be,' I said even though I knew the batteries were new. 'I've got spares somewhere.'

It mattered not. We were making good progress. We'd done some six and a half miles already. I had a quick delve in one of side pockets of my rucksack for batteries and pulled out the Peddars Way guidebook instead.

I put it straight back. We didn't need it.

The night before, in the simple shelter of the bungalow at Burnham Overy Staithe, we had talked about a scenario to play with on the walk.

'Just to pass the time, really,' I'd said.

In order to step into those prehistoric boots, we would try to imagine, as we plodded on for mile upon mile, that we were two brothers, or cousins, or close kin of some kind from those vital years that marked the very start of the Bronze Age, about 2300 BC.

Understandably, Paul seemed to frown a little.

'I mean,' I stuttered. 'Just as a bit of a laugh; a way of trying to get into the mindset of those who walked this path in prehistory.'

I continued to talk, knowing I was starting to waffle.

'Not that they would have walked exactly this route,' I said, leafing through the accumulated maps of the Peddars Way seeking our start point at Knettishall Heath. 'I mean, obviously not if it's really a Roman road.'

On the table, the three OS maps lay unfurled, covering the worn lino. On top of the maps sat a scattering of books, many of which had already travelled with me to South Uist and back that summer.

Paul laughed.

'So ...' he said slowly. 'Period dress?'

I laughed.

'If you want.'

I'd found the book I was after. It was a children's book titled 'The Bronze Age'. I turned to the first page:

Bringer of Gold

Occasionally an invention comes along that completely changes the way that people live. Around 4,300 years ago people in Britain learned how to make and work with metal. We call this the beginning of the Bronze Age.[*]

The book was part of a series called 'Britain in the Past', full of short, digestible chunks of facts about the Bronze Age and lots of colour photos. I'd seen it in the children's section of Halstead library and got it out on my daughter Molly's card.

It was the photo of that skeletal figure I was after – the Amesbury Archer.

---

[*] Moira Butterfield, *The Bronze Age* (London: Franklin Watts, 2015), p. 4.

'There.'

There was a blur of brown from which some bones could be made out and a body lying in the earth surrounded by specks of white chalk. There wasn't that much to see. But then, no one looks that impressive dead and rotten.

The Amesbury Archer.

He was one of the Beaker people – that cultural collective who appeared in prehistoric Europe from around 2500 BC and seemed to be the first to work with metal. Beaker people were defined by the style of pots they were buried with. The Amesbury Archer had been buried around 2300 BC with five such funerary pots. When he had been found in 2002, he had been nicknamed 'The King of Stonehenge' – for the wealth of his grave goods and the proximity to Stonehenge of his burial both in date and distance. His collection of artefacts to take into the next world included clothes, pots, tools and arrowheads for hunting. There were also copper knives, stone wristguards to be worn against the action of the bow string of his arch and, finest of all treasures: gold. There were two small rolled shards of gold – most probably hair tresses. They were the oldest known pieces of gold ever found in Britain.*

I showed Paul the colour photo in the book.

'Wow,' he said.

---

* www.wessexarch.co.uk/projects/amesbury/introduction.html (last accessed 19 Nov 2015)

Those fragments of worked gold were a wonder in themselves. The photo showed a band of gold wrapped around a semi-circle of gold sheet that had been rolled together and seemed to have ornamental markings etched around its rim. The object reminded me of one of those metal clasps used to secure dreadlocks.

But there was one further fact about the Amesbury Archer that made his burial in prehistoric Britain so significant. He was not British. Analysis of his teeth showed that he had spent his childhood in the Alps. He was European. At some point in his life, he had migrated from continental Europe to Britain.

Paul and I would pretend to be two sons of the Amesbury Archer. We would be British-born early Bronze Agers who were leading a new wave of metalworking across Britain. We would be part of those spreading the word of wondrous new things to the furthest corners of Britain. We would be heading to those who ran the port at Holme, where wooden seahenges marked the route across the water from one chalk ridge to the other. We were bringers of change. We were Bronze Agers stepping into a land of stone, into the heart of the flint industry of Britain which had been centred here for millennia. Here in the Brecklands of Norfolk, the finest quality flints were sourced and worked and carried north up to Holme where they could be shipped out over the Wash to Lincolnshire and on to northern Britain or away on boats that steered about the sunken isles of Doggerland and took the flint away to other worlds, other lands that were barren of this vital stuff of stone age tools.

In my mind, the scenario was swirling into fantasy. The only problem was that early Bronze Agers wouldn't have been walking this road – they would have used the winding route of the ancient ridgeways that criss-crossed Britain. The arrow-straight path of the Peddars Way wouldn't actually exist on the prehistoric map we would have been carrying in our heads. Nor would the sons of the Amesbury Archer really be working with bronze. It would be a few more generations before the shift from copper to bronze would occur. And then there was the fact that the seahenge discovered on the beach at Holme dated to around 2000 BC.

Still, it was just a game.

We headed on. Our walking boots kicked up flint fragments from the exposed earth. We strode the straight road north, edging the Merton Estate and light-heartedly playing with our 'sons of the Amesbury Archer' scenario, walking on until the path had become fenced in on either side. Then we hit a B-road.

'Fancy a break?' I said.

Thankfully, Paul agreed. I inched the rucksack to the ground beside a wooden fingerpost that read Peddars Way.

We snacked and rested for a few moments. A dog-walker passed by with an aged Golden Retriever. We passed pleasantries.

'So where are we?' Paul asked.

I retrieved the guidebook from a side pocket. The B-road was the Brandon Road.

'Erm,' I said.

According to the map, we should have had fields before us. Instead, we had a string of suburban bungalows.

'Erm,' I repeated.

It took a while and two minds rather than one to work out what had happened. We had marched on past a left turning just over a mile back. We were on the fringe of a market town called Watton. So now we had to walk back another mile or so along the B-road in order to rejoin the Peddars Way.

Two more miles added to the tally.

We set off again, now walking on paving stones. On the tarmac of the B-road as the pavement vanished we were forced to dodge speeding cars for half a mile on the long road to Little Cressingham. From now on, I resolved to carry the guidebook in my hand.

'Back on track,' I said as we finally slipped off the tarmac on to rough grassland.

The reality was that the modern-day route of the Peddars Way was a compromised one. It was obvious really. The dead reckoning of that Roman road ran through people's front rooms and the fields of unfriendly farmers. Instead, a path of best fit had been created when the trail was formed in the 1980s. In sections, it followed the actual *agger* of the Roman road. In other parts, like this, it rather meandered away. I checked the map. We were heading west. I frowned. The ancient Peddars Way ran NNW. Though back on the modern-day Peddars Way trail, we were sailing forty degrees off the correct compass direction for Holme.

'Mmm.'

We reached the village of Little Cressingham and swung back to north. I still clutched the guidebook. We had done fourteen and a half miles – not including that two-mile detour to Watton. Now the road rose gradually before us. We marched on, now silently for another mile or so, struggling to keep to anything like the pace we had been maintaining, even though the farm road was metalled under foot. Halfway up Caudle Hill, Paul halted abruptly.

'Look at that,' he said.

On the tarmac lay a snake.

'Grass snake, isn't it?' I said.

'Yeah,' agreed Paul.

The snake was tiny.

'I thought it might be a slow worm, it's so small,' he added. 'But it's definitely a grass snake. There's that white collar on the neck.'

He leant over and pointed.

'They're normally more yellow.'

The snake didn't move.

'It must just be a young one,' I said.

Paul remained close to the ground. He touched it gently with a forefinger. It didn't move. He rose to upright, the rucksack rolling on his back. For a moment we stood in silence above it, staring down at the still creature. Its body was curved in a peculiar wave that made it look a little like a six-inch long question mark on the road.

'You think it's dead?' Paul asked.

'Hasn't moved, has it?' I said and bent lower. 'I guess it could be playing dead.'

Paul took a photo and we left the being be. It was only a few days later, when I looked at that photo, I realised that the snake's body was pointed north, the neck and head orientated perfectly along the line of the ancient trackway towards Holme and the seahenge. I did some checks. Grass snakes do commonly practise *thanatosis* or playing dead. But what I couldn't confirm was whether that particular individual creature was pretending to be dead or really was.

The day was marching on. The sun now sat on my left shoulder. By the time we reached North Pickenham there was only an hour or so of sunlight left. We halted and sprawled across a welcome bench beside a farm. A rusty tractor sat between two huge silos. I unlaced my walking boots, tugged them off and then peeled my socks from my feet. It was becoming hard going. I retrieved the guidebook.

'Right,' I said, trying to sound unfazed. 'We've done nineteen and half miles.'

We both knew there was a pub marked at North Pickenham but we also both knew we hadn't reached anything like halfway. We both knew that halfway was at Castle Acre – another seven miles on.

'So,' said Paul. 'We could pile on to Castle Acre but we'd get there in the dark and then have to find somewhere to camp as close to the path as possible and only then head to the pub …'

'Or if we halted close to here,' I started.

My feet were killing me already. Even the prospect of a ridiculous figure like thirty miles for tomorrow's walk seemed better than walking on through the night.

The matter was solved by two passing locals. The pub in North Pickenham had shut two years back. They were heading to a new 'pop-up' pub that had just started in the village hall. Our hearts lifted.

'Come along if you want,' they offered.

The only problem was there wouldn't be food. We could get that well-earned pint but we'd have no supper.

'Mmm,' I said. 'That's a shame.'

It was. We needed food. We wouldn't make it to Holme tomorrow without a great big pub meal to keep us going. I had my heart set on eating a lamb.

There was one other possibility. We could walk on some three more miles and then pitch camp in a field just off the route of the Peddars Way. We would be able to reach there before sunset and so put up the tents in sunlight, or rather the dying embers of.

'See there's that pub marked at Sporle,' I pointed out to Paul.

It would mean a half-mile detour to the pub and the same back to the tents but at least we'd be rucksack free.

Paul got going at trying to reach some semblance of the Internet out here, seeking a phone number for the pub. I stared closer at the map.

'It should be perfect for camping there. No houses anywhere near.'

We packed up with renewed enthusiasm. Paul's initial search had revealed a second pub in Sporle. He had no signal to call either though. But things were looking rosier, even if that included the western horizon. The day was dying.

We marched on again, or rather hobbled for the first few hundred yards, steeling feet to the task. To distract from my increasingly painful heels, I turned back to our imaginary Bronze Age scenario.

'So we are carrying some of the first Bronze axe heads in Britain,' I said.

'OK,' said Paul.

We had left North Pickenham and were back among the fields. We were also back on the Peddars Way proper, on the true Processional Way of the Romans – even if we were pretending to be from well over two thousand years before the road was built.

'We've brought them all the way from Wessex,' I continued.

'OK,' said Paul a little more slowly.

Bronze axes must have been viewed as incredible when first seen by prehistoric people only used to stone. They had both extra precision and cutting strength over traditional flint axeheads. And when brand new they shone like sunlight. Most significantly, the new bronze version didn't splinter and break. The trees that were cut down to form seahenge at Holme had been felled by bronze axes. Because each axe had been individually forged, each cutting edge could be individually told apart by microscopic analysis of the cut-markings on those oak trunks that had formed the seahenge at Holme around 2050 BC. Such precise scientific methods meant archaeologists could state that fifty-one different bronze axes were used in working those giant oaks into the wooden henge.*

---

* Francis Prior, *Britain BC* (London: HarperCollins, 2003), p. 267.

Paul and I had leapt on a few hundred years. We were musing instead on the appearance of bronze swords.

'Didn't people just start killing each other?' asked Paul

'It must have bloody mayhem,' I said.

We wondered together how so suddenly across the society of ancient Britain, the ability to produce a sharp, long splint of toughened metal must have altered everything. That brutal killing technology that arrived with the bronze sword had never been seen before. That line of thought, of a kind of evil brought into mankind by the appearance of the first implements that could sever in one blow a man's head from his body, in turn led our talk to the violence that can be inflicted by man upon man and, soon, before we knew it, we had crossed the last miles of the day and were close to seeking a place to hide away for the night.

'That's the road to Sporle,' I said, suddenly realising where we had reached.

'Brilliant.'

A gap in the hedge beside us opened to an empty field. The sun was setting beyond in a flurry of murderous reds.

It was perfect.

Within minutes we had our tents up in the fringe of the field, a few feet from the Peddars Way. We were well hidden from any farmer's eyes. Paul was lighting his battered Trangia stove. I turned back from the sunset to the sight of the methylated spirits aflame, pouring purple fire out into the darkening night. We would have a tea and then stroll down to Sporl for a pint and a lamb.

It was Mum who'd told me of the Blood Moon. Then Paul had mentioned it when he'd popped round the other morning.

'You know there's this Blood Moon,' he'd said.

I hadn't until Mum had mentioned it the night before. The conjunction of a full lunar eclipse and what is called a Super Moon had somehow passed me by.

Now, we both sat back on tired haunches, sipping tea and staring at the vast white celestial object that sat in the dusk of the southern sky.

'So what's a Super Moon?' I asked.

I'd meant to look it up but hadn't got round to it.

'Something to do with being a full moon and a Harvest Moon, isn't it?'

It hardly seemed to matter at the time. Food and beer were more pressing. We zipped up tents and nipped back through the hedge, not needing head torches to find our way. The moon was huge already.

We walked with a new-found lightness to our step along the Sporle road, dropping down the incline of Bunker's Hill where the trees shrouded the moonlight. Our chat was light too. The darkness of Bronze Age weaponry was replaced with thoughts of the supper menu.

'Lamb for me,' I said.

Paul laughed. He was thinking beer.

'Of course a local beer should be available ...'

'Wherry?' I asked.

'Don't see why not,' said Paul.

We reached a T-junction and turned north. I didn't need the map. I'd memorised the way to the pub. Sporle was lit by the odd streetlight. A stream ran by the side of the road, channelled in parts into a stone culvert and covered by pavement. It was eerily picturesque in the moonlight. A solitary car passed.

'Seems a little quiet,' I said, more to myself than anyone else.

There was absolutely no one about. I checked the time. It was only just gone seven in the evening yet it seemed as though it was just past midnight.

The pub appeared suddenly before us. It was bathed in darkness. We both stood stock still and stared. The Peddars Inn was shut. There really was no getting away from it. A chalk board left outside declared that the pub had shut at six but it had only been serving food until three anyway.

For a little while, we both just stood and stared.

'Mmm,' I think I said, though it might have been a little stronger.

Once the reality had nailed itself down, there was the small matter of water to source. We were entirely out.

'Check round the back,' suggested Paul. 'They might have a tap.'

They did at least have that. So instead of beer we drank water at the pub. Then we filled the empty bottles we'd brought along.

In some strange way, it seemed that on that walk undertaken on one of the ancient highways of Britain to touch a sense of life in prehistoric times, we were being shown some of the more basic aspects to living that really were so easy to forget in twenty-first-century Britain. To survive, all humans needed food and water. There were other things, of course, such as shelter and warmth and love and perhaps even the respect of others. But first there came food and water. If it was a lesson, it was one I certainly didn't want to be having at that time. A lamb shank and a pint would have been far preferable.

Instead, we traipsed back through the ghostly high street of Sporle followed by the echo of our footsteps before turning into the dark inclines of Bunker's Hill, and then up and out from the houses and the trees into the ashen moonlight. In some other strange way, the fact we did now have water made things so much better. Without, we'd have had to go on until we found some. I'd pictured having to knock at some isolated farmhouse's front door to be greeted by the violent barking of dogs.

We had water. We could get a tea when we got back. We'd already started to laugh at the situation.

'At least we saw Sporle by night,' joked Paul.

Back by the tents, the stove was soon alight. Paul produced four small pots of porridge he'd earmarked for breakfast. I had a bag of nuts and two more bananas. But it was the porridge we turned to for supper. September was nearly done and a stream of autumn cold seemed to seep across the field. In the south, the moon was round and proud and had risen to forty-five degrees. It was only later I discovered that a Super Moon was when a full moon took place as the moon came near to its perigee, the point in the moon's orbit when it was physically closest to earth. The moon we were witnessing in a field in Norfolk was a Super Moon because it would become a full moon only one hour after reaching that lunar perigee in its orbit. The combination effect accounted for its vast round presence.

Moonlight lit the field. I sat on the sandy soil feeling the cold seeping in. I couldn't move. We'd walked two more miles on the Sporle adventure, making our day's total at least twenty-five miles – four of which had been utterly unnecessary. My feet were feeling it.

'I forgot,' said Paul. 'I've got a present for you.'

He produced a plastic instrument that looked just like a spoon in the moonlight. Torchlight revealed a fork.

'It's a spork,' he declared.

'Brilliant.'

It really was.

For supper we ate hot porridge from plastic pots with our plastic sporks and joked about the parallels between the revelatory technology of Bronze-casting three thousand years back and our civilisation's delight in plastic. The moon grew ever greater. At some time after two in the morning, partial eclipse would commence as the darkest form of earth shadow – the umbra – began to cross the moon. Soon after three, full eclipse would begin as that dark earth shadow entirely enveloped the moon. Earth's atmosphere extended fifty miles into space and played with the sunlight beyond the shadow to cause the colouration that turned the moon to blood red.

We talked for a while in whispered tones under that pale globe of the effect that eclipses must have had in prehistory.

'That's why you needed to predict them,' I said.

I told Paul the tale of how, many years ago, in a room in a small museum in the town of Antigua in Guatemala, I had gazed from beyond a glass wall at the folded sheets of a Mayan codex and how I had returned to that room day after day until I had copied out a single page of those archaic

symbols that recounted the predicted dates and times when
Venus would appear. Ancient societies invested heavily in
seeking knowledge of the celestial world. We knew from
such monuments as Stonehenge how much the late Neolithic
people of Britain had valued and recognised the summer
and winter solstices. Only a month or so ago, on my way
back from South Uist, I had pulled off the motorway and
taken lunch at the standing stone of Long Meg who stood
by her stone circle of daughters. Long Meg had been raised
specifically to mark the shortest day of the year – the exact
moment that the sun sank into the Cumbrian hillside on the
winter solstice.

We turned in to our tents. It had been one hell of a day.
I tucked down into my sleeping bag and lay cocooned and
gently warming. My feet ached. I closed my eyes. I thought
how I was lying on a north-to-south axis with the moon
rising steadily above my feet in the south and how in a few
short hours that snowy white orb would turn to blood. I
thought too of the poet John Clare. He had made an eighty-
odd-mile walk from Epping Forest to his home village of
Helpston in the Fens in the summer of 1841. Clare had kept
a brief journal of that journey. He wrote of sleeping such that
his head, like mine, lay to the north, while his body acted
as 'the steering point' that told him which direction to walk
the following morning as he made his way along the Great

North road.* Tomorrow, we too would walk north.

Though dog tired, I could not sleep. I turned and drew up plans for the future in my notebook then dozed and wondered if I shouldn't try to stay awake to witness the celestial spectacle due to unfurl in some four hours' time. Three a.m. was a forbidding hour. It was the witching hour. I thought about the walk tomorrow and sought sleep.

At 2.20 a.m. I was awoken by the need to wee. Outside the tent, the night was cold. The moon still lay to the south, blushed with grey shadow that was creeping into its north-western corner. It was the start of the eclipse. I could hear voices from what seemed a hundred yards or so away, back down the track of the Peddars Way that I thought must be those of farmers from nearby also out to witness the lunar eclipse. I returned for a glimpse of that blood-red moon at 3 a.m. The voices were still there. The lunar eclipse had turned much of the moon to liquid brown. A single band of light still poured from its southern edge. I shivered in the cold and stayed a moment more.

In the morning, Paul told how he had got up a few moments before me, and how he too had heard the voices.

'Sort of over there?' I said and gestured back across the hedge-line south.

---

*   John Clare, 'Journey Out of Essex', in *John Clare's Autobiographical Writings*, edited by Eric Robinson (Oxford: Oxford University Press, 1983), p. 157.

'Yeah,' he agreed.

'Hard to tell, but a hundred yards or so away?'

'Yeah. Something like that.'

Who they were, we never knew. But in the broken, misty sunlight of morning as we supped hot tea and gazed over the map I realised Grange Farm was far further than I had imagined, a good half a mile away south. It was peculiar now I thought of it but even though I had distinctly heard those voices from over the field, I hadn't been able to make out anything at all that they were saying, hadn't actually caught a single word they had said. Neither had Paul.

We packed up and walked on. My rucksack seemed to have put on weight overnight. There would be no marching today. There were twenty-two more miles to Holme. My feet were a mess. A mass of blisters had arisen in the night. Both heels ached like hell. The lack of sleep wouldn't help with the walk, nor would the lack of food. Breakfast was a bruised banana.

But the day was dry. For a hideous few hundred yards we both hobbled along until the pain in our feet had dulled down. The map had revealed we had camped at eighty-two metres – one of the high points of the Peddars Way. It was all downhill from here to the sea at Holme, we told ourselves. We passed the deserted medieval village of Great Palgrave with hardly a glance. Our path wove us off the arrow-line of the Roman Peddars Way that ran east over Hungry Hill but we eventually reached Castle Acre, stepping round the ford through the River Nar, and uphill to find coffee at The Ostrich.

'Need this,' Paul said.

Paul seemed to be doing better than me, though I could tell even he was finding the going hard. We drank our coffees and ordered more. I checked the book. We had twenty miles to go.

'Mmm,' I said.

Broken down into a pace of four miles per hour meant we would be there in time for tea on the beach. But there was absolutely no way we were going to manage four miles per hour today.

'Say we go at three ...' I said, slowly working it out in my head. 'Erm ... then we would still be there before sunset.'

It was a straw to clutch at. We sat there on a bench sipping coffee with sunlight now breaking through. The physical effort of those thousands of footsteps really wasn't appealing. I felt sick.

At a local shop, we loaded up on supplies and once more found our feet. The ancient road ran dead straight from here for the next seventeen miles or so. All we had to do was manage to walk it. I'd hatched a plan to dump the tents in a secluded hedge.

'We can pick them up tomorrow on the way to Thetford.'

It made a difference. Something shifted from the seemingly impossible to the just feasible. We walked and we walked.

For much of that journey we walked in silence. I tucked back inside myself and started counting steps as I often did when walking alone. It was a form of ritualised practice that seemed to arise involuntarily. If a form of meditative process on better days, then today it was one of necessity that took me away from the present and the pain in my feet to a place just adjacent where I could cope and could walk the next step and the next and the next in a monotonous plod that would get me from here to Holme.

'One, two, three, four, five, six, seven, eight.'

I counted each footstep I took. Then I repeated the sequence and marked each count of eight on my fingers. When I had reached thirty sequences of eight, I began again.

It seemed the only way.

I thought of that oft-quoted Latin epigraph: *solvitur ambulando.*

It is solved by walking.

So on we walked – proceeding along that section of the Peddars Way marked on the map as a Processional Way.

There was a fresh breeze and clear, warm sunshine pouring from Magritte-clouded blue skies. The wonders and delights of that Norfolk countryside of rich, brown, ploughed or sheep-strewn fields passed us by on that glorious day so perfect for walking. Though the day was ideal for a stroll to the sea, I can only look back on those hours as a nightmare. Though I had planned and prepared for that walk of the Peddars Way for weeks and begun the walk with glee, much of it really wasn't enjoyable. Some weeks on, I sat and talked it through with Paul in The King's Head.

'There was ... like a siege mentality,' he said. 'It was a route march.'

'I mean, I really thought we'd be fine with the mileage,' I said.

'I know,' agreed Paul. 'I did too. It wasn't the distance. It was the route. It became a slog; an endless, straight march.'

They were my thoughts precisely.

The very nature of the Peddars Way was surely to blame – that arrow line that sliced through the soil; not meandering with the contours of the chalk hills and rises, the streams and rivers but tearing against the grain of the landscape. There was a brutality in imposing a route through the countryside that seemed to have somehow reverberated through time until we too felt the harshness of that unearthly imposition. In so many ways the Peddars Way symbolised and exemplified the division of two ways of living on the land. That pure clarity of constructing the shortest way from A to B that formed the rationale for the Roman road network contrasted so clearly with the ancient roads of Britain that already existed and that wove their way in sympathy with the landscape. Those green tracks were 'winding ways' and something in that motion made them far more congenial to walk. I returned to Edward Thomas's *The Icknield Way*:

> Probably these twists, besides being unconsciously adapted to the lie of the land, were, as they are still, easeful and pleasant to the rover who had some natural love of journeying. Why go straight? There is nothing at the end of any road better than may be found beside it, though there would be no travel did men believe it. The straight road, except over level and open country, can only be made by those in whom extreme haste and forethought have destroyed the power of joy ...

While the pathways of the pagan folk of Britain – villagers, people of the earth, of nature – flowed through the land, the roads of the Romans – urban, city-dwellers, people of commerce – tore through the land, especially if those lands were foreign, merely wild wildernesses at the edge of empire. In the very roads they travelled, so the ancient British mindset could be told apart from that of the Roman.

---

* Edward Thomas, *The Icknield Way*, p. 5.

It was only weeks later, too, that I realised how our imaginary game of being two sons of the Amesbury Archer – British-born Early Bronze Agers – would only ever have worked on the gently meandering ancient path of the chalk ridgeways. On the Peddars Way, we were not Bronze Age master archers, born to the bright, new Beaker people and bringing our wondrous bronze-cast wares to the folk of Seahenge who ran the boats across the Wash. Not at all. If we had been anyone from the ancient past, we had to have been Roman soldiers – *milites* extracted from some distant home, some distant realm of the empire to march through these Iceni heartlands in order to maim and murder all before us. We would have been Roman soldiers sent to put right the apparent wrong that Boudicca and her Iron Age warriors had done to the Roman cities of southern Britain. *Solvitor ambulando* took on new meaning. The re-organised military might of Roman Britain would have walked north along the Peddars Way to solve the problem of the Iceni and their allies for ever more. And so if we were to have been any ancient figures walking that roadway in some imaginary game, we would be Romans on a march of bloody revenge for Boudicca's Revolt. It was rather a shocking realisation when it finally came and yet in some strange way it explained much.

We walked on. At some point on that seemingly endless straight drive we rested beside a copse of trees and I lay and stared up through the bare branches of a stag head oak to the blue sky. Before us, pock-marking the fields of grazing sheep, were the tumuli of Bronze Age burial mounds. From the map, I saw we were at Harpley Common. The tumuli lay all about us – round circles lifted from the land to hold the bones of some ancient beloved souls lost to death.

'That's a wayfaring tree,' said Paul.

I looked over. Paul was looking to a shrub behind us.

'*Viburnum lantana.*'

'Nice.'

I smiled and we laughed.

'Odd that it's here,' said Paul. 'They come from southern Europe. Imports.'

So we mused a moment if some Roman hadn't brought a seed upon his boot two thousand years before and that here before us was the sole surviving shrub from generation after generation of wayfaring trees that had grown up here beside the Peddars Way. We laughed again, a little deliriously. We were both killing time before we had to rise and take the pain of stepping forward once more. It felt so good to stop walking but that delicious sense of ease was tainted with the knowledge that we must soon walk on again.

I had already checked the book. There were still thirteen miles to go.

We turned in to ourselves for the next few miles once more. I counted steps obsessively and mindlessly, tallying the hundreds on my fingers and tossing them to the wind and starting again; footstep after footstep along that brutal pathway as on we went through the monotonous field-scapes on our ever-fixed mark. We stepped past ancient villages: Anmer to the west, then Fring to the east. Then we inched up a vicious incline to Dovehill Wood. Close to Sedgeford, I thought of the hundreds of prehistoric torcs that had been found in the nearby fields – each forged of twisted cables of gold and silver to be worn about the neck. Many, many moons ago, I had spent a week on an archaeo-logical dig there in Sedgeford, passing my days in a Saxon burial pit, scraping mud from the bones of the long dead, before carefully prising each bone from the soil for reasons I could not fathom. One day, I had stepped up and out from the pit and had been stopped stone dead by the sight of an amber Saxon bead sat upon the surface of a trampled patch of earth.

I turned my neck west towards Sedgeford but walked on north. There was no time for treasure hunting today.

'One, two, three, four, five, six, seven, eight,' I counted steadily in my head.

At Ringstead, we stepped from the soil track to the tarmacked streets. My feet screamed. Yet there was now a sense of so nearly being there. Through the village, a finger-post pointed us round a field and declared a single mile to Holme. We walked west a while. The low sun flickered in my face, scattering through autumn leaves. It was done. Even if I fell here, it was downhill. I could roll.

We laughed again and emerged through a thicket on to the coast road. The beach and the sea were straight ahead. So was the site where Seahenge had stood four thousand years before.

'Do you want to go on?' asked Paul.

He knew my answer.

'It's not there, is it?' I said.

So we wove off east instead, along a lane that led us past wild, unkempt hedges and flint-walled houses until we reached a red sign on a white-washed wall that said The White Horse. And the front door tinkled as it opened before us and we stumbled in with our rucksacks still upon our backs and, though heads turned, we smiled and laughed. And there was fresh beer on tap and lamb shank on the menu.

And on the wall above the fireplace was a large picture frame that held a black and white photograph of Seahenge whose shrunken oak pillars were still being washed by the waters of the North Sea.

GOLD

I stand in an empty field. It is autumn. Rain has fallen for much of the day and now a little drizzle fills the dusk twilight. Mud – born of the alchemic action of rain on earth – has now formed and sticks to everything. Mud covers my Wellington boots from the heel to the toe and up to the shin. Mud has spread in streaks and patches all the way to my trouser pockets. Mud has sodden my knees, while the gloves I wear on my hands hang heavy and cold with more mud. I should have gone home an hour ago but instead I stay in this field of mud and stare down at the muddy hole that I have dug. I frown and wonder if even now I should just fill the hole and leave. But, of course, I will stay. I lift the instrument beside me and sweep it over the ground, the fringe of this Essex field, and back over the six-inch wide space of the hole.

'Beep,' it says loudly to the dank airs.

And then as I sweep it back over the hole in the same fluid motion, only reversed, it perfectly echoes the noise from the very centre of the hole.

'Beep.'

I kneel. The damp muddy patches on my knees are cold against the earth. I place the instrument carefully on the ground beside me, pick up the trowel and dig deeper, lifting lugs of soil up into the half-light, turning them to the spoil heap that has formed beside me and digging down again, deeper still until the hole is eight, ten inches deep. And with each inch further down in the earth, I dig with ever-greater care and concern, awaiting the touch of metal on metal. Yet still it does not come.

I lift my head and, still kneeling, rest my muddy hands on my muddy trousers. My heart is beating fast in thrilled anticipation. It really might be.

And when I next dig down with the trowel, there is that distinct sound of metals touching. I throw the trowel aside and scrape at the mud with my muddied, gloved hands until something shines from the soil. It is hard to tell in the dying embers of the day but the metal really does seem to glint, to gleam.

I lift my head again and scramble to find a stick, a twig, to work the soil from around the object to reveal more of the metalwork.

'It's ten inches down,' I remind myself and think of archaeological context, wonder if the time to call a halt is now, yet continue edging the earth away in scrapes until there is a twisted structure of exposed metal visible at the base of the hole. The stick snaps in two. I dig on with the larger twig until I feel the object shift and come free from the earth and I can lift it to the light.

I really had thought, an instant before, knelt there upon that field, a lone figure in the dying light, that it really was the gleam of gold that I saw rising from the soil. For more than a moment, the crushed metal really did seem to mirror the fragile frame of the Ringlemere Cup. Instead, it was a tin can. Quite how a can had managed to worm its way ten inches beneath the surface I could not say but it was for certain a tin can and not a prehistoric gold cup. Yet it is that lure of gold that will ensure my return to a muddy field in autumn. It is the lure of gold that keeps the lone figures of detectorists plodding so very slowly over the furrows of ploughed fields, metal detectors swinging gently before them. It is the dream of seeing that untarnished gleam peering from beneath, from far beyond. That is the unifying hope of all detectorists. Only a handful have witnessed that moment, have felt the thrill as they have seen the gleam, have held gold freshly dug from the earth. All have imagined that moment.

In the late autumn of November 2001, in another muddy field in southern England, another metal detector beeped. But that beep wasn't for a tin can. I had read about the moment in a book called *Hidden Treasure*. The detectorist was a retired electrician called Cliff Bradshaw. The beep he heard was distant but distinct.

He scraped the ground with his foot and tried again. The signal was still very faint, but the sound had increased. There *was* something, though deep. Several times … he dug away the earth and tested again with the detector, gradually closing in on the target …

It was the narrative of a hunt. The hunter and the hunted locked together in a moment of high tension. The prey was cornered. The seeker was now so close. Even the metal detector became a primal creature in this scenario.

... instead of a low growl the machine was giving off a high-pitched whine: that meant something non-ferrous ... Normally with a tin can – the most likely non-ferrous 'discovery' – the audio screams at you and the meter goes off the scale.*

Except, Cliff's machine didn't scream. From more than a foot deep in the ground, Cliff saw the gleam of gold. He had just found an Early Bronze Age gold cup – soon to be named the Ringlemere Cup after the area of Kent where he was standing. Until that moment, only one such gold cup had been known in Britain. Now there were two.

It was the kind of moment that I had been dreaming of since the age of twelve when I had finally managed to buy my first metal detector after endless months of saving up. It was really just a section of black plastic with the most basic of electronic wiring, but it worked and made a satisfying enough beep to keep me entertained in silent bliss for hours. I can still see myself meandering steadily over the wasteland edge of the Thames beside my grandparents' houseboat, occasionally extracting rusty nails from the earth. My greatest discovery had been the silver thimble I found a year or so later in my Uncle Arthur's garden in Hertfordshire, scratched and squashed but distinctly treasure. But even then, I hadn't

* Neil Faulkner, *Hidden Treasure: Digging up Britain's Past* (London: BBC Books, 2003), p. 32.

been that exhilarated by my find. It was gold I was after. And really it was ancient gold. Not some gold wedding ring lost in the park, but something from the distant past, something truly beautiful that had been worked by a goldsmith thousands of years before and that had lain in the darkness for an age until I had been the one to let the sunlight fall once more upon its surface and I had been the one to see that gleam as the gold shone again.

Gold lust seemed to run through time, as if there existed some kind of cultural continuity across the world where gold is concerned. The desire for gold seemed ubiquitous. Thomas More wrote of gold lust in *Utopia* back in 1516. More portrayed a land so endowed with gold it no longer has a value: iron is the sought after metal. When emissaries from the Anemolians arrive in *Utopia* they are amazed at the gold, at:

> so vast a quantity of gold in their houses (which was as much despised by them as it was esteemed in other nations), and beheld more gold and silver in the chains and fetters of one slave than all their ornaments amounted to …[*]

---

[*] Thomas More, *Utopia* [1516] (Cambridge: Cambridge University Press, 1989), p. 77.

That Golden Fleece which Jason and his Argonauts were after might well have been born from the fact that sheep's fleeces had been used from prehistoric times to catch gold washed from alluvial deposits by a technique called placer mining. Think too of that gold mask laid over the mummified body of Tutankhamun. Or of Montezuma's gifts of gold to the Spanish conquistadors that only fuelled their greed for more Aztec treasure. That can be seen as a collective form of gold rush fuelled by imperial greed. The gold rush in California from 1848 involved a more individual lust – thousands of hopeful treasure hunters came from across America heading west as news of gold nuggets spread. They were soon followed by hundreds of thousands more from across the world.

It seems we all want gold.

In the years when I first moved to Essex, I would drink and play pool in the local pub with a gold dealer called Ron whose gold rings I can still picture emblazoned against the green baize of the pool table. It still seems the most exotic of jobs. In the early 1980s, I had been ecstatic when my Dad had announced that he had bought some gold coins.

'Krugerrands, they're called,' he had said. 'From South Africa.'

Obviously, I had wanted to see them and though they were kept in the safe in the bank, Dad had agreed that he would one day soon get them out to show me. He shared my gold lust. And I remember him some time later, returned home from work and standing beside me, opening a pale white envelope that held – was it two, or three? – thick gold coins. Yet I cannot remember holding one. Perhaps it was because even then I knew a modern bullion coin held so much less allure than something ancient or something plucked by my own hand from the earth. Perhaps Dad had the same feelings too, or perhaps it was to do with apartheid, but he sold the coins soon after.

Some months back, when I had first met Howard Davis on the trail of the Roman Road, he had been keen to show me his finds from his years of metal detecting. They were carefully collected in labelled trays and cases. Part of me had always yearned for such an approach to my finds. He had happily brought his treasures to the kitchen table where we were having a cup of tea and poring over nineteenth-century maps of the local area. I lifted a round brass bell from a box containing a dozen or so siblings. I shook it and a chime rang out across the kitchen.

'Crotal bell', said Howard.

Apparently, they weren't uncommon finds.

I shook it again and another wonderful song of sheep and shepherds and spring rang out from the eighteenth century.

'They wore them on horse harnesses,' said Howard and I saw instead a great Suffolk punch striding across a muddy field to the sound of brass bells ringing.

The trouble was that I had always really been rather a bad metal detectorist. I had all the enthusiasm and desire for both the process of researching and the glory of finding things but not the patience to spend those endless hours waving the coil head back and forth, back and forth over the ground. Yet every few years the desire to find some fragment of the ancient world would return to me. It had done so when I had moved to the wilds of Essex and first acquired the field. I'd gone out and bought a new metal detector with a new-found enthusiasm to know what was beneath that earth I now owned. Over one autumn, I'd systematically covered the ground. At the very edge of the field, closest to the green lane that ran beside the cottage, I'd found that Roman coin. That find had kept me going for a while but the truth was that until I met Howard this summer I hadn't used my metal detector for years. Howard, on the other hand, was a very good detectorist. He loved the research and he passed those hours in the field with a patient expectation for the next find. He also rebuilt my machine when it wouldn't work after years of not being used.

'I'm an electronics engineer,' Howard said as he handed back my metal detector. 'I love fixing machines.'

Then he started to text me about digs.

James

We're meeting at 1.30pm just past Monks Lodge towards Chelmshoe.

Bring Wellies. Could be sticky.

Later, Howard

I was becoming a detectorist again. I started to dream once more of turning the soil and seeing the gleam of gold – perhaps one of those Iceni gold coins: far rarer than the silver ones yet still decorated with that flowing, stylised form of a leaping horse on one side.

And then I learnt of something that was also made of gold and that was far older, far more wonderful even than Iceni treasures. They were called sun discs. They were circular pieces of prehistoric gold that had been worked and decorated, often with the most intricate and beautiful of designs by the hands of the first metalworkers. Archaeologists often officially called them 'flat discs' as the term was 'more interpretatively neutral'.* But to many, and to me, they were sun

---

* Stuart Needham and Alison Sheridan, 'Chalcolithic and early Bronze Age Goldwork from Britain: New Finds and New Perspectives' (p. 908), in *Metals of Power – Early Gold*

discs – round and gold just like the sun. After all, gold had always had a sense of being a physical embodiment of the sun. Even the Latin term for gold, 'aurum' meant 'shining dawn'. Yet only thirty-three sun discs had ever been found in Britain and Ireland, though others had been unearthed across Europe. Most of those from these isles had been discovered in Ireland by people out cutting peat who had seen a bright and mysterious sunlight shining from the depths of the bog as the turf spade dug deep down into the distant past. Most sun discs dated from the Early Bronze Age, though some came from a rather earlier period of prehistoric time known as the Chalcolithic – a Latin term constructed in the late nineteenth century and literally meaning 'copper-stone' age. The term referred to a Copper Age when copper and other metals such as gold were being worked just before bronze had been first forged. Each of the sun discs found across Britain and Ireland could be dated to between 2400 BC and 1800 BC – each gold disc was some four thousand years old.

It is the sight of one that spellbinds. I saw my first sun discs in the British Museum and was instantly mesmerised. There were four on display. Each was distinct in size, shape and style of decoration. Each shone. The artificial light of the museum gallery caught the gold edges of embossed

---

and Silver, Tagungen des Landesmuseums für Vorgeschichte Halle, Band 11/II 2014.

metal. The intricate, delicate decoration of each disc had been painstakingly punched into the flattened gold surface four thousand years before. It was just staggering really. I bent down on my knees and the light shifted on the gold of the discs, flickering, catching different corners of the decoration. The smallest sun disc was perhaps two centimetres across. The largest and most stunning of the four was two inches in diameter. Round the outer rim of the gold circle ran a concentric ring of embossed lines, a pattern which was repeated in a second, smaller concentric ring that centred the sun disc. And inside that inch-wide ring pattern was a cross form whose arms tapered out slightly in a manner that reminded me of the ankh of ancient Egypt. I stared from beyond the glass.

That sun disc had been found in a place called Kilmuckridge, County Wexford, in Ireland. I pictured the scene on the day of discovery – a peat bog on a dull, autumn day suddenly lit by a glimpse of sunlight rising from the turf. The information board stated:

Decorated sheet-gold discs are found mostly in Ireland. Two burial finds in Britain suggest that they were worn on the head or upper body; some have been found in pairs. The decoration, made by impressing the surface on one side, is often based on a cross within a circle.

For some moments, I continued to bend and sway before those sun discs so that the light played upon their surfaces. Then I caught sight of something else in a neighbouring glass case that momentarily tore my attention from the sun discs: that Neolithic stone treasure from the Outer Hebrides that had bounced about my mind for much of August – the Benbecula ball.

I started to think of Ireland. Or rather, I started to think of prehistoric Ireland and of Irish gold. I kept picturing a scene on a peat bog and a pair of sun discs unearthed by the turf spade. An online search threw up a tasty-looking report titled 'Archaeologists discover evidence of prehistoric gold trade route between Britain and Ireland'. A summary of the study was even more intriguing:

Archaeologists at the University of Southampton have found evidence of an ancient gold trade route between the south-west of the UK and Ireland. A study suggests people were trading gold between the two countries as far back as the early Bronze Age (2500 BC).

The lead archaeologist was named as Dr Chris Standish. Within an hour I had his article on my desk. It had only been published six months before. I felt like I'd been given privileged information on an extraordinary scientific discovery.

The title of the paper was 'A Non-Local Source of Irish Chalcolithic and Early Bronze Age Gold'. At least I now knew what Chalcolithic meant. I turned and started reading.

> The brilliance of gold, its colour and lustre alongside a resistance to tarnish, have afforded this metal a special role in societies irrespective of time and place.[*]

I then turned back to the summary that I'd skipped because it had begun with the phrase 'lead isotope analyses'. I skimmed through. Essentially, the point was that whereas an assumption had always been made in the past that Irish gold artefacts from the Copper and Bronze age had been made from gold sourced in Ireland, in fact geochemical analysis suggested that the gold most likely came from 'the alluvial deposits of south-west Britain' – i.e. Cornwall.

I read on.

---

[*] Christopher D. Standish, Bruno Dhuime, Chris J. Hawkesworth and Alistair W.G. Pike, 'A Non-Local Source of Irish Chalcolithic and Early Bronze Age Gold', *Proceedings of the Prehistoric Society*, Available on CJO 2015 doi:10.1017/ppr.2015.4, pp. 1–29 (p. 1).

The wealth of Irish gold artefacts from prehistory had led to that running hypothesis of a local source. It made sense. The alluvial deposits of County Wicklow and then those of the Mourne Mountains in County Down were considered as likely sites for the gold. There was a picture of gold oval plaques, their intricate design and beauty evident even in the grainy black and white printed photo. I read that over eighty gold lunulae – those flattened necklaces shaped like a crescent moon – had been found in Ireland. That was 75 per cent of all gold lunulae ever discovered – 'the remainder scattered along the Atlantic facade of north-west Europe'. I turned the page and there was one – a gold lunula from Rossmore Park, County Monaghan. Again, despite the grey of the photo, the glorious effect of the gold somehow still shone. The intricacy of the embossed patterning was still remarkable. It was so easy to forget these were made four thousand years ago.

I reached the section sub-titled 'The Lead Isotope Signature of Irish Gold Mineralisation'. The reading got thicker. A lot of elements, or rather isotopes of elements, started to appear within the sentences. My comprehension started to fade. I reminded myself I'd once studied chemistry and plunged back in only to be lost in a whirl of isotopic signatures.

So instead I rang Chris Standish.

He was a lot easier to understand. We talked gold.

'You can find gold all over northern and western Britain,' he said within a few seconds of us chatting. 'It's more common than you think.'

Instantly, I imagined texting Howard and suggesting we head west with our metal detectors on the trail of real treasure – gold nuggets. I held off.

Chris explained how there was further work to be done in Wales in particular, such as at the Clogau mine, and in as many places as possible where gold had been sourced, to build a more comprehensive picture of the pattern of prehistoric gold usage in Britain and Ireland. Then there was the matter of Irish gold and the now-outdated hypothesis that prehistoric gold came from Ireland because there were so many ancient gold artefacts in Ireland.

'You could see how that happened,' I suggested.

'Sure,' he agreed. 'I mean, do you know of the Wicklow gold rush?'

I didn't but I looked it up soon after.

In 1795, gold had been found in the Wicklow Mountains. Prospectors had flocked in seeking gold in the alluvial deposits of the river that was soon renamed the River Goldmine. Some eighty kilograms of gold were found within six weeks. One gold nugget weighed in at 682 grams. The gold frenzy continued until the government intervened and took over the enterprise in 1796.

We continued to talk gold. Events such as the Wicklow gold rush only served to strengthen the assumption that ancient Irish gold came from Ireland. The abundance of gold in Ireland was clear. One obvious question remained unanswered. Why use Cornish gold? It really was impossible to say. In the paper, the phrase 'cosmologically driven acquisition' had been used as a possible scenario – 'the deliberate procurement of a material from distant or esoteric sources' – as to why Cornish gold had been favoured over local Irish gold. I had frowned when I read that. It didn't make much intuitive sense. Surely you'd use the local gold?

I had meant to ask Chris that question but instead we got sidetracked on another subject: metal detecting.

Historically, relations between archaeology and metal-detecting hadn't been good. The academic establishment of archaeology had traditionally seen those wielding metal detectors as mere fortune hunters, as hooligans only after hoards while archaeology dug into the earth to seek layers of history, to carefully uncover the truths of the past. Yet archaeology also had a streak of gold lust in its genes. Howard Carter's tale of digging in the sands of Upper Egypt in 1922 and of finding the tomb of Tutankhamun and spying 'wonderful things' illustrates how archaeology and treasure-hunting have always been intertwined. Of course there were a few detectorists who would still search sacred archaeological sites under the cover of dark – the dreaded 'night hawks'. But the truth was that most of those who quartered the fields of Britain with their detectors like divining rods were also fascinated with ancient history.

Chris was talking of the Bronze Age gold finds made by detectorists – like the Ringlemere Cup.

'Are you a detectorist?' I asked with mock interrogatory tone.

'I've never held one!' Chris laughed. 'I'm more of a geochemist. Mass spectrometers are more my thing.'

Chris was busy enough leading a vital aspect in the future of archaeological research – employing the science of isotopic analysis to redefine our knowledge of goldworking in ancient Britain and Ireland. But he was also sympathetic to the notion that metal detectorists hadn't been recognised for what their finds had done to enhance our knowledge of ancient Britain, especially in the Chalcolithic and Bronze Age.

'Have you read that article on metal detecting that was published a couple of years back in an archaeological journal?' he asked.

'No,' I said.

'I'll send it,' Chris said.

And he was true to his word. A few moments later, I was sat at my desk with a recently published article from the German archaeological journal *Archäologisches Korrespondenzblatt*. Fortunately, it was in English. The title was

'What have Metal-Detectorists ever done for us? Discovering Bronze Age Gold in England and Wales'.

For the moment, the matter of detectorists and Bronze Age gold would have to wait.

The chat with Chris had me thinking of further fields.

A week on, I stand on the final few feet of Cornwall before the land falls into the sea. I look north. Somewhere out there, Ireland lies beyond the grey cloud, way beyond the invisible horizon. The water below looks cold and angry. I try to see signs on the waves of those distant travellers from four thousand years ago who crossed this stretch of sea seeking gold. I too have come to these lands in the south-west corner of England to search for gold.

There had been a sense of *Lorna Doone,* or, rather, a Cornish version, to my arrival the night before. I had arranged to stay with a friend, John Fanshawe, whose family had lived in these rugged Cornish lands for generations. John had grown up in the stone fortress I finally arrived at after driving for hours from the east of England. We both shared the same rather cavalier, holistic approach to directions and finding your way, trusting more to instinct than sat-navs. He'd given me his address and I'd headed for Boscastle in Cornwall and then after six hours had parked up in Boscastle to discover a text message from John with further directions to his home. It had all felt rather deliciously Le Carré. I had followed my nose out of town then plunged down a steep track as directed.

It really was pitch black. I dropped through an avenue of blackthorn and emerged to the sight of John framed in the impressive majesty of a doorway forged from dark, local rock. Behind him rose a small castle built of the same imposing stone.

Even as I greeted John on the threshold of his Cornish home, the lesson in the use of local materials had struck me. The contrast to my own home was immediately obvious – stone versus wood. My cottage had been built for farm labourers around the same time, some four-hundred-odd years ago, yet not of slate and granite, but of oak and wattle and daub – of hair and muck and mud. And yet, I had just travelled hundreds of miles musing on the question of why prehistoric Irish goldsmiths had used Cornish gold when they had a source of gold on their doorstep. It seemed so illogical.

John and his family offered food and friendship and warmth. There were stone fireplaces and stone floors and then a spiral staircase that was also made of stone up to my bedroom. In the morning, John and I walked out across the

fields to the cliff edges that marked the north coast of Cornwall, snaking a path along a V-shaped slice into the bedrock
called the Grower Gut until we stood at the land's end among
stubby blackthorn thickets and brambles and gorse bushes.

'Great blaze of yellow,' John said.

He was right. Against a day of greys, dressed with a touch
of rain, the gorse flower was stunning.

'So where exactly is Ireland?' I asked.

We had halted on the very last few feet of England. Beyond
was a drop of a few hundred more feet down into the waters
of the Irish Sea. Even today, without too much wind or rain,
you really wouldn't fancy making that crossing – especially
not in a Bronze Age boat.

'Sort of over there,' said John, pointing out into the cloud
on the horizon.

He used his arm as a kind of compass needle, swinging
it to the east where an island could just be made out against
the gloom.

'That's Lundy,' he said.

We'd been chatting on the stroll over as to the route those
intrepid prehistoric gold hunters would have taken from
Ireland. One way would be to head straight for Cornwall
from somewhere like Cork in southern Ireland. That would
be about three hundred kilometres, pretty much all at sea.
Or you could make the sea crossing from, say, Rosslare to

St Davids in Wales. In contrast, that would mean less than a hundred kilometre sea crossing. Surely that made more sense. Then you could make your way down the coast in a series of shorter voyages – working around the West Wales coast to Pembroke and then straight south across the mouth of the Bristol Channel for Cornwall. Yet that was hardly a safe route either.

'They might even have stopped off there,' I said. 'On Lundy. Good source of birds' eggs.'

John had been a leading figure in bird protection for decades. I wondered if it was rather an insensitive reference. But John didn't seem to mind.

'Mmm,' he said.

He was still musing on Lundy.

'I lived there for some months as a teenager,' he added rather wistfully. 'Ringing birds.'

We wandered back past black-faced sheep. The land was touched with the bronze tinge of dead bracken leaves, an autumnal sheen on the northern edge of the land as I glanced back towards the sea. It really was such a voyage to make – from Ireland to Cornwall. Even in summer, with warm winds from the south-west and a bag of bartered Cornish gold aboard, and a steady route round the coastline to where the crossing was shorter.

John brought me back from my imagining.

'See those dark peaks in the distance,' he said. 'That was where Thomas Hardy met Emma Gifford.'

I halted and turned back.

'See that cattle shed,' John said.

'Yep,' I agreed.

'The high ground beyond is Beeny Cliff and then High Cliff.'

Hardy had travelled here in March 1870 from Wessex, as a young architect under instructions to restore the collapsing church at St Juliot. He met Emma Gifford as she rode a pony across these cliff-top, coastal pathways – a place he later called 'the land beyond the land'. It was another of those wildly Romantic Cornish tales, retold in Hardy's novel *A Pair of Blue Eyes* in 1873 and then again in poetic form following Emma's death in 1912. Hardy had returned to these lands in March 1913. 'Beeny Cliff' was one of a poignant series of poems he had written of their first meeting on these wild shores:

O the opal and the sapphire of that wandering western sea,
And the woman riding high above with bright hair flapping
   free –
The woman whom I loved so, and who loyally loved me.[*]

---

[*] Thomas Hardy, *Selected Poems* (Oxford: Oxford University Press, 1992), p. 29.

The rain had started to set in. We walked back inland. John told of his own youthful wanderings along those cliff-edge paths, mainly on the trail of peregrines. I glanced back. Cloud was starting to cover the edges where land met sea.

Back outside the imposing frame of his home, I said my goodbyes to John and headed on south for Truro. As I wove my way along rock-edged roads, my thoughts turned again to gold, and to those Bronze Age hands that held it in their palms. That was where I was headed – to find a nugget of Cornish gold.

It is an inch in depth, a little more than an inch long. It shines with the dull glow of gold. It can be nothing but. I lean in to see the series of smoothed bulbous gold bumps that surround a series of pale quartz crystals. The gold looks as though fluid, as though it was in liquid form and suddenly frozen. It is a gold nugget. There in my hand. And I am not dreaming.

'So this is from Ireland,' the voice beside me says.

I hold Irish gold.

'Wow,' I say.

I look at the man who has handed me this lump of gold ore. I feel its weight in my hand. Apparently, it weighs an imperial ounce. He smiles. I hand back the nugget and feel the lightness in my palm. Then he hands me another nugget of gold.

'And this one is from Cornwall,' he says.

I hold the nugget of Cornish gold.

I am dumb-struck.

It is native gold.

This gold nugget is heavier in my hand. It shines with a far finer light, glowing with sulphurous-yellow intensity. Rather than a rough lump recently plucked from the ground, this is pure gold. It is perhaps three inches long – a sinuous and misshapen chunk of sunlight. I gaze closer. There are signs of edges and surfaces. It looks as if it was once worked and then partially melted down once more. You can see the mark of man on the gold. It is as though it were once formed into a bar – a perfect bar of gold.

'Wow,' I finally manage to say.

After a while it sits warm in my hand. When I unfurl my fingers, it has an allure that makes it hard to hand back.

But hand it back I must. Michael Harris is one of the curators at the Royal Museum of Cornwall. He takes the nugget back. I struggle a little more with words as I thank him for that moment. Yet Michael can empathise. Though he is a fine art curator, the Carnon Downs nugget has often caught his eye from its exhibition case.

'I've passed it so many times before,' he says. 'And wondered how it felt.'

Now we both know.

The gold goes back in a box for the moment. We are deep in the archives, in the vaults of the museum. Tomorrow it will be back on display. But today it has been in human hands.

Before I left, Michael presented me with copies of their archive records on the two gold nuggets and then we shook hands with a delightful sense of a secret shared. He returned to work and I turned to those archival outlines of the gold. Both nuggets of gold were what was described as 'water-worn'. Their smoothness came from their riverine existence ever since they had broken free from the lode or vein of ore where they were born. The Cornish nugget had come from a few miles down the road at Carnon Downs, a long-aban-doned alluvial tin mine, worked from many centuries before. The Irish nugget had been found at Croghan Mountain in County Wicklow. At some time, that Irish gold nugget had then travelled here – a journey in the opposite direction to that made by the Cornish gold nugget which had somehow sailed to Ireland in prehistoric times.

Later that day, I met Anna Tyacke. Operating as part of the Portable Antiquities Scheme under the wing of the British Museum, Anna was the Finds Liaison Officer for Cornwall.

'I love gold,' she said with a great smile.

It turned out her husband was a goldsmith.

'When it comes out of the ground after hundreds, thousands, of years ... there's no tarnish.'

Anna dealt with a lot of detectorists. She presented me with a leaflet on the Portable Antiquities Scheme and guided me upstairs to an exhibition case of local finds.

'I get a lot of phone calls from people who start the conversation with "I've just found some treasure",' Anna explained.

The display case was a finds table for 'Cornwall Unearthed', a metal-detecting group whose blue-and-white badge was also on display. Anna pointed me to a small strip of gold ribbon that had been found recently by detectorist Graham Dyer. It was more prehistoric Cornish gold. I stared through the glass. At one end, there was a small puncture hole – a tiny round space in the sea of gold that told of the action of some hand from prehistory.

I was developing gold fever. Over lunch, I turned back to an article that Chris Standish had sent me. I had already read through it a number of times. It was by Mary Cahill, curator of the National Museum of Ireland in Dublin, the home of a remarkable collection of prehistoric gold. The article was titled 'Here Comes the Sun ...' It had appeared only a few months earlier and explored solar symbolism in the

Early Bronze Age. She detailed the variety of the designs these discs of gold held:

Some discs have a combination of plain rings alternating with zigzag lines with or without central cross motifs, whilst others use angled rays to form a sort of whirligig motif.

Illustrated images showed a series of elaborately patterned sun discs that included crosses, concentric rings, rays and dots in a variety of combinations. A few days before, I had had one of those moments of revelation when I had realised just how similar the two-pound coin was to a sun disc – and to one disc in particular: a button cover found at the Knowes of Trotty on Orkney, Scotland which had a series of concentric rings containing a cross hatch design of zigzag lines.

But it was Mary's article that really opened my eyes to the significance of sun discs. She argued that though the patterns were widely ranged, these gold discs could be grouped 'to form a loose typology'. Their 'common aim' was 'to represent the sun in forms that are visible to the naked eye'. In prehistoric times, people observed the movements of the sun through daily and seasonal variances. 'For example,' she argued, 'watching the sun going down over water produces a number of visual and colour effects that have been observed for millennia.'

Mary Cahill's point was that the sun discs were designed to show how the sun was seen – both by prehistoric eyes and by our own.

In this way the use of a cross can be understood as representing a sun where the rays appear to extend from the centre to form four arms. This is frequently seen at sunrise and sunset. On some discs the arms of the cross are laddered ... perhaps mimicking the effect of the reflection of the setting sun on water. *

Exactly so.

One of the sun discs where this effect of laddered light is shown in the arms of the cross was illustrated in the article. It was one of a pair that had been found at Kilmuckridge, County Wexford at some time in the mid-nineteenth century. One of those golden twins was now in the National Museum in Dublin. Its sibling was the very sun disc that had held my attention for so long in the British Museum.

It was only when I returned from Cornwall that I got back to the matter of metal detecting and Bronze Age gold. The

---

* Mary Cahill, 'Here Comes the Sun ...' *Archaeology Ireland,* Spring 2015, pp. 26–33 (pp. 27–8).

article which Chris Standish had sent me had the wonderful title of 'What have Metal-Detectorists ever done for us?' with that mock-voice of the outraged archaeologist. But there was a rather more serious tone immediately adopted in the narrative:

> Archaeologists have only slowly started to realise the research potential of the thousands of new finds generated each year by metal-detectorists ...
>
> This slowness by archaeologists stems from a traditional and often strong antipathy towards metal-detecting.[*]

The implementation of the Treasure Act in 1996 and the Portable Antiquities Scheme – piloted in 1997 and then rolled out across England and Wales in 2003 – had meant a huge rise in the number of recorded finds of ancient gold objects. In just thirteen years from 1997 to 2010, one third of all known Bronze Age gold artefacts had been discovered – all thanks to detectorists. There were the grand finds like the Ringlemere Cup but also hundreds of other single gold items. Each Bronze Age find made by a detectorist and reported under the Portable Antiquities Scheme meant a 'find-spot', which

---

[*] Alessia Murgia, Benjamin W. Roberts and Rob Wiseman, 'What have Metal-Detectorists ever done for us? Discovering Bronze Age Gold in England and Wales', *Archäologisches Korrespondenzblatt*, 44 (3), 2014, pp. 353–367 (p. 353).

could be subsequently explored by archaeological investigation. Not only was the gold item brought to light but its context could then also be studied.

In fact, the truth was that since records had been made of the earliest finds all the way through to the present day, 'only 17 of the 371 findings [of Bronze Age gold] were made during archaeological excavations'. The reality was that our knowledge of Bronze Age gold came not from the work of archaeology but from the labours of others:

The overwhelming majority of Bronze Age gold discoveries found in England and Wales have been made by farm labourers and other ground workers, antiquarian excavators, and metal-detectorists – not professional archaeologists.[*]

It made sense but it was also good to read it in black and white – and in an archaeological journal. It was amateurs who had always brought Bronze Age gold to light. Detectorists were merely a modern incarnation of the eighteenth-century antiquarians who had done so much to lay the ground work for the subject that would become known as archaeology.

I thought of that glorious sun disc that had held me rapt in the British Museum. Mary Cahill had just sent

---

[*] 'What have Metal-Detectorists ever done for us?' pp. 358–9.

me some more material that detailed how that particular sun disc and its twin had been found 'near a great stone cross' at Kilmuckridge in what was then County Waterford. They had subsequently been bought in 1840 by Mr Redmond Anthony who Cahill described as 'innkeeper, collector, dealer and amateur antiquarian'. Anthony had possessed a 'custom-made bog oak case' in which he kept his remarkable collection of Bronze Age gold artefacts. They were part of his own 'museum' at his home at Piltown, County Kilkenny. For a small entrance fee (that was donated to a local 'Fever Hospital'), visitors were welcome to view this collection. After his death in 1848, Redmond Anthony left not only his artefacts but an archive of letters that provided details about the provenance of many of his antiquities. One letter, dated 14 April 1840, was addressed to a fellow antiquarian and collector called George Petrie and told of Anthony's recent acquisition of the Kilmuckridge sun discs:

… a few days ago I got at Enniscorthy a pair of splendid ones [sun discs, or 'thin plates of gold' as Anthony called them] and send you a rough sketch of one, the other being precisely the same, both weigh nearly ½ an oz. and 3 inches in diameter. Indeed, I believe they are the largest as yet found and as all such things are pure gold … and have a very imposing appearance. I know they imposed on me.*

Over a century and a half later, one had certainly imposed on me, too.

What Mr Anthony wouldn't have known, and nor had anyone else known until a few months ago, was that the gold from that stunning three thousand year old slice of Bronze Age sunlight had come from a far distant corner of Cornwall.

---

*   Mary Cahill, 'Mr. Anthony's Bog Oak Case of Gold Antiquities', *Proceedings of the Royal Irish Academy. Section C: Archaeology, Celtic Studies, History, Linguistics, Literature*, Vol. 94C, No. 3 (1994), pp. 53–109 (pp. 53 and 63).

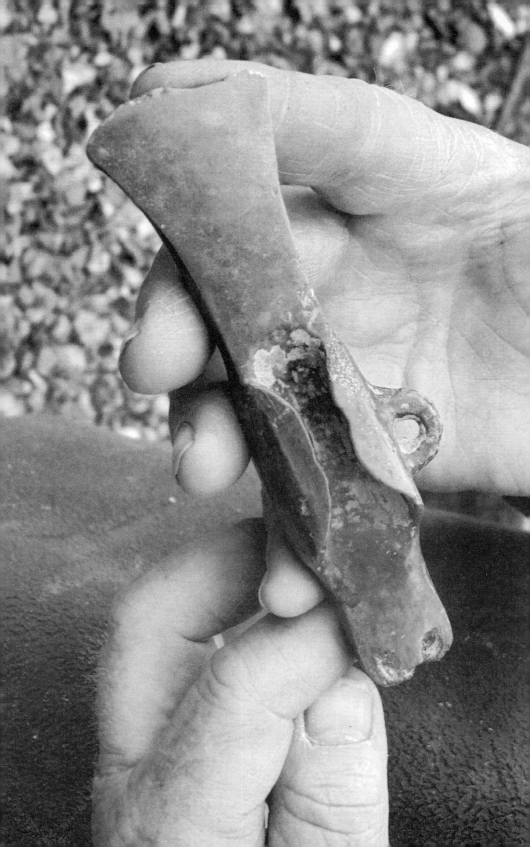

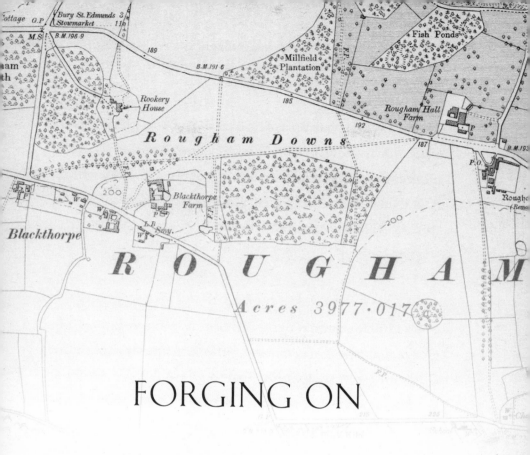

FORGING ON

I stare into the fire. Yet this fire is like no ordinary fire. This fire has not been lit to warm or to cook, or to comfort. A brilliant, orange glow radiates from this fire. This is a fire that burns with a heat that will transform, that will melt all laid before it – for in truth, this is not a fire but a furnace. There is a steady intensity to the fire of the furnace that is fierce, frightening. From the mouth of the furnace, a sinuous absinthe-green swirl rises and rests above the flare. I bend low. At eye-level height I can better watch the small green cloud as it morphs and shifts through a subtle spectrum of colour changes: from emerald to jade; then on to a tinge of mossy, turf green; now to a vaporous verdigris. That miasmic, green swirl is strangely mesmerising as it dances in the air above the circle of fire. And then I see that sea-green, pea-green phantom for what it truly is: it is the genie of the furnace.

It is a chill, autumnal Sunday morning. We are gathered in glorious, deepest and darkest Suffolk. At an old smithy in a hidden glade are four fortunate souls who have spent the last few days as apprentices in alchemy. I have stepped into their world, into this outhouse, to witness the ancient ways that they are gradually learning. Each apprentice is keenly focused on their tasks – they hammer and drill with bodies still, with heads fixed on the objects of their attentions. The material burning in the furnace is malachite – a copper ore from which the metal can be leaked out in the heat. Then, when that copper is added to tin, the two combine in the fire to form bronze.

We are here to cast bronze. Yet for the moment, I am still held by the genie who plays above the furnace. In substance, this apparition is a heinous mix of arsenic and other evil elements that leave a cruel lick on the tip of your tongue and the back of your teeth. I am here at the invitation of Will

Lord. He oversees all and guides me away from the fire, out into the fresh air beyond.

'You'll be able to taste it by the end of the day,' he says. 'A horrid metal tang on your tongue.'

I had rung Will the week before.

'I've stepped back into the Stone Age,' he had declared. 'The Bronze Age was killing me.'

At first, I had thought that he was joking. He wasn't. The arsenic released from the smelting of malachite to produce copper really does kill – it would have gradually poisoned Bronze Age metalworkers, too, as they proceeded in their alchemic ways. And so within minutes of talking to Will, I was already looking back on what I knew of Bronze Age Britain with new insight. I thought of Cladh Hallan and remembered the small round outhouse that sat just to the east of the middle roundhouse. And now I saw it for what it was – a sheltered workspace in which to forge bronze. Crucially, it was separate from the main roundhouse that held the family. The poisonous genie could be contained.

Outside the shed, Will leads me to another basket of fire in which lies a mould. When the time is right, he will lift the urn of molten copper and tin and pour the bronze alloy into that mould. We step back into the shed and stare down to the molten bronze in the furnace. The surface of the metal has now become clear.

'The first mirror,' Will says.

If I braved the heat I would be able to see my own face. But the heat is fierce even from standing height. I peer over into the glare and see the swirling vortex of the bronze, the slick sheen of the surface.

Simon is Will's able assistant at bronze-casting. He tells me more of the science of the process. Tin makes up around ten per cent of the bronze and has a melting point of 232°C. Copper, on the other hand, which makes up the other ninety-odd per cent, has a melting point of 1084°C. When the two metals are mixed, the melting point drops to around 950°C.

'But you want them to flow,' says Simon.

He is missing a front tooth. He also has an infectious enthusiasm, a bright friendly face and an impish way. His long pointy beard is neatly matched by a pointy leather hat.

'You see, you need to overheat to get a good flow rate,' Simon explains. 'So you heat to 1200°C or so.'

The gas-jet furnace is rather more modern than a Bronze Age metalworker would have had. They would have needed a couple of hours of using a bag bellows to reach such temperatures.

We both look down once more into the molten mire. It feels like staring into the heart of a volcano. In a way, it is. Simon ventures an iron rod into the furnace to draw off some slag from the surface. I look down again. The bronze mirror is perfectly clean.

It is time. One of the other apprentices steps forward. He is a local man called Peter who I had been chatting to earlier. From a coat pocket, he had produced a double-sided and socketed Late Bronze Age axe. He had placed it in my hand. His brother had found it in a field in Germany while out metal detecting. Now Peter is primed and ready to cast his own Bronze axe.

The noisy buzz of the electric tools is stilled. There is a wonderful silence to the moment as the molten bronze is lifted from the furnace and gently poured into the mould. As it flows from the beaker it really does look like liquid sunlight. Then the mould is taken outside and placed in the gentler heat of that secondary furnace, the basket of fire, where the bronze can gradually harden into the axe-shaped form of the cast.

There is the chance to step back a while. Will leads me to the quiet of a wooden shed he has transformed to a museum of flint. He is a kind man who has already generously given his time. Now he talks me through the ways of flint from the earliest tools of the earliest days of the Palaeolithic through to the most intricate and incredible flint blades of the late Bronze Age. The collection of flint implements are displayed on shelves around the hut. Some are finds. Many have been made by Will.

Will's father is the famed John Lord who moved out to the lands of East Anglia in the 1960s to become the guardian of Grimes Graves – the most significant flint mine in ancient Britain. John Lord had then taught himself the ways of flint-knapping until he was a world expert in stone technology. He had virtually invented experimental archaeology before the term had ever been employed. John now understood more about prehistoric flint use in Britain than any one – except perhaps for his son Will. John and his wife Val had brought up Will in a way that was unique. Will had been raised in the grounds of Grimes Graves. As a child, Will had the run of the wide heath plains of Norfolk's Brecklands and the forests of Thetford. He had the freedom of the flint mines as his playground. And he had learnt the ways of prehistoric peoples from a young age, as though they were part of the present.

A few weeks earlier, I had walked those scarred plains of Grimes Graves with my daughters Eva and Molly on the last day of the half-term holiday. Even on a day of drizzle and grey cloud, they'd both wanted to run about the hillocks of the ancient mine-workings excited as young rabbits. We'd climbed down the ladder into the dark gloom of the underground and shared an intriguing delight in doing so, in staring into the tunnels dug from early Neolithic times to mine the flint seams in industrial quantities. We had happily crawled and scrambled about in the half-light below ground, getting dirtied with streaks of mud and chalk in an odd mimicry of those distant Stone Age miners. And then an hour or so later, after returning to the surface of the earth and October daylight and strolling over the in-filled shafts and pits of the five-thousand-year-old flint mines seeking flint while being steadily soaked by a Norfolk form of smirr, Molly and Eva had pleaded to be allowed to step back down the ladder into the darkness. I could hardly have refused.

That was the world Will had grown up in. And now he happily spent his time sharing the knowledge he had gained of life in ancient Britain. From his home here in the wilds of Suffolk, Will ran a variety of prehistoric courses: flint-knapping, tanning, longbow and arrow making workshops. He even offered a 'family prehistoric survival day' with a 'prehistoric lunch included'. Yet it seemed I might well be at the final bronze-casting workshop.

We walked back over to the heat of the basket of fire. It was time to open the cast that hopefully held Peter's bronze axe. Will was experimenting once more – this time with the material of the cast.

'In the past, I've used clay,' he said. 'And really fine sand with a little bit of dung.'

'Right,' I said.

'And for this one I've used grog,' Will said.

I had to ask.

'What's grog?'

'It's clay that's been fired and then crushed quite fine.'

He pointed to the variety in the clay particles that made up the cast. The process of experimentation was essential to practical learning. I caught a glimpse of Will there beside me, bearded and long-haired, wearing his leather jerkin and standing before the charcoal fire. It suddenly wasn't too hard to peer back in time to Bronze Age ways. Not when you had Will testing different materials for casting axeheads.

'So what was the thinking behind using this crushed grog?' I asked.

'The trouble with the sand is that it starts to turn into glass,' Will said. 'And so instead of the moulds being stable, they start to turn to toffee.'

'And this is the first time you've tried this way?

'This is the first time with the grog,' said Will. 'And the outcome has been substantially more secure.'

'Wow,' I said. 'So in a way you're mimicking what they would have done. Trying different ways, as any practitioner would do.'

'Yeah,' agreed Will.

I looked back at Will and realised that here was someone who really did have an insight into the ways of prehistory.

He really did. Not by digging about in the sites of the past but by being actively engaged with living by prehistoric ways. Will was also the only person in Britain who had a generation of prior prehistoric knowledge passed on to him by his father. Will was raised prehistoric. He was also very skilled at calmly analysing the process he was undertaking.

'For a long time we've been smelting the malachite and getting a variety of outcomes. We've had ball bearings and these wiggly ingots which were really clear copper and then this weekend we've had these copper outcomes that look a bit like a biscuit.'

He retrieved a rusty piece of fragment from the worktop. It did indeed look rather like a biscuit. It wasn't really the outcome you wanted from smelting malachite. But Will was already working on a new technique.

'What you really need is carbon particles to bond to the malachite particles and separate the copper. So we've seen a system which is pretty much a lazy-day's work: you dig a little hole in the ground. You put your malachite in, you put your charcoal in and then you cover it over to reduce the air getting in there. So it's a bit like making charcoal. You give it a couple of hours, gently bellowing and take it out and you've got a decent ingot.'

Will looked at the copper biscuit in his hand.

'Because to get that after a whole load of successes ...'

He paused a moment.

'But then you start to think about other questions. Like, what are those white bits?

I looked closer at the mesh.

'Yeah, what are they?'

'Dunno,' said Will.

He thought a moment.

'They could be bits of a leg bone actually. There was a bit of bone about when we restarted the fire from embers. So it could be bits of bone particles.'

Simon was in the process of lifting the lid on the outdoor furnace. Will stepped closer and with tongs extracted the cast. Peter closed in with a hammer in his hand. He steadily worked the grog casing off in fractures and fragments until the remainder was the rough outline of an axehead. There was a soft blue tinge to the object. Peter took it away to be worked on.

I asked Will if he ever got the chance to talk with other metalworkers.

'Like blacksmiths?' I suggested.

He had but only after having spent a long time working on his own, experimenting and revising practices and processes along the way.

There couldn't have been that many people who he could talk to.

'The problem is that the bronze-casters who have established a reputation, a name for themselves – not all of them but certainly some – they defend their knowledge very well. They like to be regarded as magicians.'

'Like alchemists,' I said.

'They don't like what I'm doing much because I'm letting the secrets out of the bag. A lot of what I do is a skilled-based scenario. So you can't flint-knap just because you've been told how to. But with this, all I need to do is show you how to do it and you can go away and do it.'

'So do you think that even in Bronze Age times, they would have kept their secrets? Perhaps passed them through their children?' I asked.

Will thought a moment. He still held the copper fragment in his hand.

'Possibly,' he said. 'I don't know.'

It was the only answer. How on earth were we to know what Bronze Age people did in terms of passing down their bronze-casting skills?

On a battered and ancient workmate bench, Peter was chiselling away at the molten grog still clinging to the copper.

'You getting there?' I asked.

He paused and looked up.

'Yeah,' he laughed. 'I think so.'

He wasn't wrong. In his hand he now held what was distinctly and definitively a Bronze axehead, and not one tarnished with a familiar verdigris patina like the one he had shown me earlier that day. This one had a fresh brilliance. It glowed with the fiery light of the sun.

'That's amazing,' I said.

It really was.

And he had smelted the copper and cast the bronze himself – with a little sprinkling of knowledge from Will Lord.

There was someone else I needed to meet. Like Will Lord, he was born and brought up in prehistoric worlds. I also knew that like Will Lord he would be able to guide me towards a greater understanding of what it really was like to be around in ancient Britain. So I headed west. I headed to a place I hadn't been to for an age.

The fleeing darkness gradually revealed it was another dank and dismal day. A misty Wessex drizzle pervaded. Yet somehow it felt like the perfect weather for my visit. I walked south along a long, straight track. Sunrise was still some moments away. A nebulous greyness covered the land through which the white chalk of the track shone clean and clear. I walked on as far as the great cursus and then halted. This vast enclosure had been dug out of the landscape by red deer antler picks in the Early Neolithic sometime around 3500 BC. It ran for 1.7 miles on a roughly west-to-east axis. And I was stood at the midway point. Exactly what it was for, no one really knew any more. I gazed along its faint outline and then turned back to the south.

A familiar cluster of stone stood before me. From half a mile away, Stonehenge rose on the horizon. In the strange half-light of dawn, the stones merged with the morning mist that lifted from the fields. I stood and watched as the stones emerged from the shadows of the fleeing night. There was a sense that these stones were somehow both solid and ethereal, as though even their very presence on the landscape was ephemeral. I walked on, closer and closer, drawn to the stones across the unkempt fallow field as light seeped into the day through the cloud cover. The land dropped and then rose once more as I approached and the stones of Stonehenge seemed suddenly huge and impressive.

I went no further. A fence barred me from doing so. A security guard in a lime-green hi-vis jacket patrolled the stones. He glanced over towards me, the only other soul around. I looked back but said nothing. Instead, I picked flints from the fresh brown soil of molehills. I crouched low against the ground and saw a string of shrunken Bronze Age burial mounds and thought of those at Harpley Common in Norfolk that I had seen when resting prone on the Peddars Way. I wandered to the east, towards the solitary molar monument of the Heel Stone where the true entrance to Stonehenge lay. The ancient processional avenue ran down the slope of the field to the east and away, off to the south-east and the site of the henge at West Amesbury.

The darkness faded. I poured a cup of Thermos tea. Then I turned to the thin book I had tucked in my pocket. It was Aubrey Burl's *Prehistoric Stone Circles*. For the best part of twenty years I had taken this book with me on various ventures around Britain. The sunlight-faded cover illustration was of Swinside Stone Circle in Cumbria. Swinside was one of the early stone circles dating from the Middle to Late Neolithic (*c.* 3370 to 2670 BC). It had been one of my first, too. Two years ago, on a journey around the Outer Hebrides, I had visited Callanish on the Isle of Lewis. It was one of the late stone circles from the Early to Middle Bronze Age (*c.* 1975 to 1200 BC). Callanish had been the last of the great stone circles of Britain for me to visit. In between there had been many days spent wandering moorlands and heaths seeking lesser-known circles of stone covered with bracken and bramble. I thought of the day I had finally seen the spectacle of the Stones of Stenness, all those hundreds of miles away north in the Orkney Islands, perched on a peninsula in a sea of lochs. It had been grey that day, too.

I turned to the pages on Stonehenge and reread Aubrey Burl's words once again as rain started to fall.

Visual effect was everything. Despite the monument's appearance of stability it was an architectural disaster. To ensure that they were of the desired height some stones had foundations that were dangerously insecure. The result was an impressive but ramshackle edifice.

Before their erection these monstrous sarcens were treated just as carpenters would have dealt with wood – smoothed, chamfered, rebated, mortise-and-tenon jointed – to imitate the ring-beams of the vanished mortuary house. It is this that sets Stonehenge apart. It was the accomplishment of woodworkers who chose to build in lasting stone. The result was the intriguing and awesome ring that looms in shattered magnificence today, a megalithic triumph.*

That it certainly was.

I drank my tea and then walked back north. All the way I felt the presence of Stonehenge behind me. I glanced back

---

* Aubrey Burl, *Prehistoric Stone Circles* (3rd edn) (Princes Risborough, Bucks.: Shire Publications, 1994), p. 39.

over my shoulders at intervals and saw snapshots of the monument as it fell away towards the horizon.

It was only later that I was able to refer to Aubrey Burl's more magisterial tome *The Stone Circles of the British Isles*. It was a far weightier book – certainly not a field guide. I had left it in my room at Sarum College, where I had stayed the night before, overlooking Salisbury Cathedral. Burl referred to Britain's most famous prehistoric site as a 'ravaged colossus'. It was a monument that had been 'wrecked in antiquity' and that now 'rests like a cage of sand-scoured ribs on the shores of eternity'.* As I read those words after returning from the stones that morning, I wondered vaguely if Burl had actually arranged the book's layout – his words on Stonehenge appeared on page 303, matching the number of the A-road which passed so close to the actual stones.

I was due at Salisbury Museum. The museum was housed in another old college on the cathedral square. Somewhere within was the man I had come to meet. As I stepped though the medieval entranceway, it was Louise Tunnard who first met me. Within what seemed seconds, Louise was talking

---

* Aubrey Burl, *The Stone Circles of the British Isles* (London: Yale University Press, 1976), p. 303.

about Thomas Hardy and *Jude the Obscure*. Her blue eyes really did sparkle as she told me how both of Hardy's sisters had been here, in this very building, for their teacher training, as indeed Sue Bridehead had been, some years later.

'Jude, of course, was working on the cathedral,' she said.

Louise turned and led me away through another grand wooden door. It opened to reveal the outdoors where a dank drizzle was falling. I followed her out into the rain.

'And that's the route which Sue took as she fled,' said Louise. 'Escaping over the backfields ...'

She pointed across the green lawn of the stone-walled quadrant before us, towards the open iron gates on the far side. It was as though Sue had only left recently. We both gazed at the gateway. I took a photo that showed the rain in splats of grey splotches. I was ready to return inside to the dry. Louise smiled.

'There would have been water meadows then,' she said and swept an arm out, as though waving Sue Bridehead off.

'We're on the confluence of five rivers, you see,' she looked at me and smiled again. 'They've been drained now.'

We stepped back inside and talked a few moments more together on all manner of matters Wessex. It really was the most remarkable introduction. Louise's passion for Hardy was impressive.

'Hardy's a pagan writer really,' I heard myself saying.

'Everything goes wrong in the town. "Stick to the fields, to the villages", he seems to be saying.'

Then I saw the meteorite.

Thoughts of Hardy vanished. The meteorite sat on a plinth in a glass case. It was actually rather hard to miss, though somehow I had managed to as I had followed Louise on the footsteps of Sue out and away into the water meadows.

'That's incredible,' I said.

'Isn't it?' agreed Louise.

It was dark brown in colour, roughly round in shape and close to two feet or so across though missing a sizeable section. Its surface was fractured by fissures that rather made it look like a great, dried ball of mud. Except it weighed in at ninety-two kilograms. I thought instantly of the Wold Newton meteorite sat in another glass case a long way away. The rock before me was called the Lake House meteorite and had landed in Britain some 30,000 years ago. It actually illustrated far better the ties between prehistory and shooting stars than the Wold Newton stone. The Lake House meteorite might even have been deliberately placed in a burial site by prehistoric hands in Stone Age or Bronze Age times. Edward Duke, a nineteenth-century antiquarian owner of Lake House, was credited with unearthing the meteorite from one of the burial mounds he had excavated nearby.

'And this is called The Milky Way Corridor,' Louise said, sweeping her hands along the gallery.

Yet I hadn't come to Salisbury to see shooting stars. The man I had come to see was in the next room. Louise led me away. We passed a painting.

'Is that a Turner?' I asked.

It was.

'We've got five Turners,' she said with a smile.

For the moment there was no time even for Turners. We walked on into a wide gallery full of fresh bright, light, passing a variety of artefacts all dug from local soils.

'Here he is,' announced Louise. 'The Amesbury Archer.'

And there he was indeed. Laid out in mock burial before me, a skeletal spray of bones surrounded by his collection of grave goods. He was magnificent, even four thousand years after death.

'Wow,' I said.

He had been found not far from Stonehenge in May 2002, buried in a wooden chamber beneath a low mound sometime around 2300 BC. He had died aged somewhere between thirty-five and forty-five years old. And there was just so much about him that was significant – both his life and death.

For a start there was that list of grave goods: five Beaker pots, eighteen arrowheads, two bracers (archers' wristguards), four boar's tusks, 122 flint tools, three copper knives, a pair of gold hair ornaments and a cushion stone used as an anvil for working copper or gold.

The gold and copper objects were the oldest known in Britain. Yet the facts about him as a living person were also fascinating. For a start there was that isotopic analysis of his teeth, which suggested he was born in the Alps. He also had a left kneecap missing, which meant he would have walked with a pronounced limp.

'And look at that hole in his mandible,' said Louise.

We leant over the glass, peering down over him at the pronounced puncture visible in his jawbone.

'They think it was from an abscess,' she added.

'Ow!' I said.

We were joined by Owain Hughes, Salisbury museum's Learning Officer, who pointed me in the direction of a small screen showing video footage of the Amesbury Archer's excavation. An archaeologist stood neck-high in the dig hole surrounded at ground level by a series of what looked like ice-cream containers filled with earth. It took a moment to recognise that the dig was taking place at night. The light was being provided by a car's headlights.

'A Peugeot 205,' Owain said.

There was a delightfully amateur feel to the dig – a sense of night-hawking to the scene.

The Amesbury Archer really was an amazing figure. His was not only one of the earliest Beaker burial graves in Britain; he perfectly represented those strong links to continental Europe that existed in the first era of metalworking. He was one of the Beaker people of Britain – named after their pottery but known for their cultural sophistication across Europe. These Beaker People had been forging new ways of working with gold and copper but also sharing common practices with funereal rites. Their pan-European scale and apparent ability to travel long distances in a lifetime made you re-imagine ways of living in that pre-Bronze Age world. Small groups of these Beaker people, like the Amesbury Archer, were responsible for bringing metallurgy into Britain and Ireland. The copper in his grave goods had been analysed some years back and shown to have come from continental Europe rather than the far closer source mined on Ross Island in Ireland. Of course, he might well have simply traded for the copper but the finding at least showed the extent of European links in that early metalworking period.[*]

I knelt down and looked in at the spread of the grave goods gathered around the skeleton before me. There was that incredible, inch-long gold hair tress. Beside it was a beautifully fine barbed-and-tanged arrowhead. It wasn't alone. There were seventeen others buried alongside.

---

[*] Andrew P. Fitzpatrick, 'Great Britain and Ireland in 2200 BC', in *2200 BC – A Climatic Breakdown as a Cause for the Collapse of the Old World?*, Tagungen des Landesmuseums für Vorgeschichte Halle, Band 12/II 2015, pp. 805–830.

He was an archer, after all. Though he had died in an era defined by the first use of copper and gold, the quantities of flint surrounding his skeleton served as an important reminder of the significance of stone throughout prehistory. Even as copper (and later bronze, and even iron) were discovered and worked, flint remained a crucial material. I thought of Will Lord's comments about stepping back into the Stone Age. Even as those fancy new metalworking skills had emerged in Britain somewhere around 2500 BC, even as they had spread and developed and been refined over the following centuries, there had always been a place for skilled flint-knapping.

'What of his companion?' I asked.

There was the matter of his so-called 'companion' who had been unearthed a few metres away, later that same year. No one seemed sure. He was certainly not on show, but then his grave goods had been rather less spectacular. Yet the companion was intriguing in that he was biologically related to the Amesbury Archer. He had died aged between twenty and twenty-five years old and was a generation or two younger than the Amesbury Archer but whether son or grandson or nephew hadn't been determined.*

---

* A.P. Fitzpatrick, 'The arrival of the Bell Beaker Set in Britain and Ireland', in J.T Koch and B. Cunliffe (eds), *Celtic from the West 2. Rethinking the Bronze Age and the arrival of Indo-European in Atlantic Europe*, Oxford, Oxbow / Celtic Studies Publications XVI, (2013), pp. 41–70.

'Think he's in storage,' said Owain.

I'd been fixed on the notion of generations ever since using them on South Uist to count back through prehistoric time. Seeing things in generations made sense. There was also the notion of knowledge being passed down the generations, a process surely only more pronounced in the ancient world. You could imagine the Amesbury Archer or any other of those early metalworkers passing on their newly emergent skills. It was exactly as with those alchemic secrets that Will Lord had talked about a few weeks back. The magical elements of the forger would only have been told to a chosen few – told to the next in the family line.

It was a model of Stonehenge that finally drew me away from the Amesbury Archer. The henge was two foot across. The stones were all upright and in place, positioned as had been intended in the final arrangement of the monument around 2200 BC. The central setting of four trilithons that made up the Sarcen Horseshoe sat surrounded by the circle of outer stones. It looked as I had seen it earlier that morning at dawn, only somewhat tidied up. There was an accompanying exhibition concerning the archaeological dig begun in 1919 at the instigation of the Ministry of Works and led by Colonel William Hawley. One of Hawley's notebooks was on display, opened to a page titled 'Aubrey Hole No. 29' and dated to 14 September 1921. I leant in to read the copperplate handwriting of Hawley's meticulous records.

We had been joined by another figure in the gallery, who I later learnt was called Anthony. He was smartly dressed in a suit and was a volunteer guide to the Wessex Gallery. A small screen was showing a black-and-white film. It was of Colonel Hawley's dig at Stonehenge in 1920. Together, we stood and watched the remarkable footage.

'That's amazing,' I said.

Men in a variety of hats and suits clambered about the monument. One smoked a pipe. Another, dressed in plus fours and tweeds, was measuring one of the fallen stones.

'That's my grandfather,' said Anthony.

I looked from him back to the grainy, black-and-white film.

'The one with the moustache,' he said smiling.

'What?' I said.

It was news to Louise as well. She'd never realised that Anthony was Anthony Hawley, grandson to Colonel Hawley who now stepped about the stones of Stonehenge with his handlebar moustache, just as he had done a hundred years before.

I turned back to Anthony and shook his hand. Here was that generational footprint once more.

It was nearly time to leave but there was just time enough to spend a moment with one of those Turners. On the wall beside me was a watercolour dated 1827 and simply titled

Stonehenge. The painting was one later published as part of Turner's *Picturesque Views in England and Wales*. Stonehenge was lit up in a dramatic thunderstorm. In the foreground a dog howls. A shepherd lies beside him, apparently struck down by a lightning bolt. It had all been rather calmer that morning.

I left the museum in a flurry of goodbyes. Louise kindly showed me back to the grand wooden entrance door, leading me back along The Milky Way Corridor where Sue Bridehead had fled for the fields. Yet it was only as I stepped out into the sunlight and the sight of Salisbury cathedral gloriously pale before me against a blue sky that I saw there really was something of Sue in Louise. They shared that same indomitable vivacity of spirit.

It was much later when I finally reached home that I was forced to return to the matter of Turner and Stonehenge. I had searched my bookcases for my copy of *Tess of the D'Urbervilles* in order to reread that end scene where Tess wanders into the stone circle of Stonehenge and when I did finally find the book I was struck by the extraordinary cover image on my old Penguin edition, which had clearly been painted by Turner. The scene showed Stonehenge as the sun was setting. The foreground was of the fields and footpaths in a dusky light, above which was a sky of spreading clouds lit with the colours of sunset: in between, stood the stones. Yet

Turner had painted the stones as though they were not solid but see-through. And by making those huge stone statues translucent such that the hills on the horizon beyond could be made out through their insubstantial shapes, Turner had painted them with that same strangely ephemeral feel which I had seen with my own eyes that very morning. It was a stunning effect. Turner had given the huge stones of the monument a delicate, diaphanous nature. I stared closer and could make out a solitary figure in the foreground who was framed against one of the pathways and I realised too that the aspect, the view or perspective, of Stonehenge sketched by Turner was the very same one that I had seen as I had walked east across that dewy, fallow field in the dawn light.

The preface to the book stated that the cover showed a detail from *Stonehenge* by J. M. W. Turner and that the painting was in a private collection. The information did little to solve the mystery. It was clearly a different *Stonehenge* from the one I had seen in Salisbury museum. I emailed Louise to thank her for her guidance and asked if she knew anything of the second Turner. Then I turned to the final pages of the book.

Tess and Angel Clare were on the run through the wilds of Wessex. They had stepped through Melchester (Salisbury) at midnight then 'followed the turnpike-road' for some miles before it 'plunged across an open plain'. The last fragment of moonlight had been soon lost behind cloud. They had ventured on though 'all around was open loneliness and black solitude' then stepped into what Hardy called a 'pavilion of the night'.

'It is Stonehenge!' said Clare

'The heathen temple, you mean?'

'Yes. Older than the centuries; older than the d'Urbervilles!'

...

Tess, really tired by this time, flung herself upon an oblong slab that lay close at hand, and was sheltered from the wind by a pillar. Owing to the action of the sun during the preceding day the stone was warm and dry, in comforting contrast to the rough and chill grass around which had damped her skirts and shoes.

...

'One of my mother's people was a shepherd hereabouts, now I think of it. And you used to say at Talbothays that I was a heathen. So now I am at home.'[*]

I left Tess to sleep on the stone of Stonehenge. It was time for me to head to bed, too.

---

[*] Thomas Hardy, *Tess of the D'Urbervilles: A Pure Woman* [1891] (London: Penguin, 1978), preface and pp. 483–4.

Things seemed to be coming together. I knew that my time was nearly up. The thing with obsessing about anything is that deep down in some distant fragment of your mind you know when that world has reached its apogee. It may be that the knowledge surfaces only in a retrospective sense yet once that moment is passed there follows a natural process of procession where the object of that obsession can gradually fade and some form of normality may steadily return. It is as with the cycle of the sun or the moon or the turning of the stars. We stand spellbound before the spectacle of the setting sun on the shortest day of the year. Then we can turn back to our daily lives knowing that each day will hold a touch more sunlight than the one before.

There were two more people that I wanted to talk to about ancient Britain. Both were based in London. The first was Mike Parker Pearson, the archaeologist who had led the work at Cladh Hallan for years. Mike was based in the archaeology unit of University College London in the glorious setting of Gordon Square. His office was suitably book-lined. He sat behind a desk covered in more books and scattered with papers. We shook hands. I said that Chris Standish, the Cornish gold analyst, sent his best.

'Chris told me you've been busy with the bluestones of Stonehenge,' I said.

'Yes, yes,' said Mike with a smile. 'Many projects.'

He was back in the confines of his office for the day yet you could tell he was happiest outside, digging about and musing on the ways of ancient worlds. I could have gladly sat and heard of Mike's latest work on Stonehenge, but I was really there to ask about the mummies of Cladh Hallan.

'So,' I said with some sense of drama. 'I guess there's really just one question: have you found evidence of mummification across Bronze Age Britain?'

Mike laughed; stretched back in his chair.

'Yes, we have,' he stated firmly.

So it was true. Mummification wasn't merely a ritual confined to a small settlement on the South Uist coast. Our Bronze Age ancestors across Britain had been routinely preserving and mummifying their dead. It was genuinely thrilling to hear.

Mike gave a little more detail. One of his colleagues, Tom Booth, had gone back and looked at all kinds of skeletons, from all kinds of periods.

'He found out it's just the Bronze Age ones that show this lack of post-mortem deterioration and decay.'

Mike seemed quite calm about the matter but then he had known about it for a while now. It was news to me.

'That's a pretty dramatic finding, isn't it?'

'Yes,' agreed Mike. 'Absolutely.'

'I mean the South Uist mummies were pretty exciting...'

'They were indeed pretty exciting. We just had the perfect context for finding it there. Beautiful machair sand made of shell so bone is immaculately preserved.'

I asked the obvious question.

'So where does Bronze Age archaeology go now?'

'Well, every now and then I give a talk to a conference in Europe and of course the key thing is a question of getting them to do this for the whole of Europe.'

Mike sipped his coffee.

'The thing we know about the British Bronze Age is that it's very much plugged in to what's happening on the other side of the channel. In the Neolithic it's a different question – they're much more isolationist. But in the Bronze Age, everyone is part of this massive metal trade – there's all this gold coming out of Cornwall but it's not just gold, it's the copper and especially the tin. I don't know if Chris told you about the isotopic analysis of tin…'

He hadn't. I'd been too fixated with gold.

'We're seeing Cornish tin going right round Europe.'

My sense of Bronze Age Britain was shifting fast. Seeing the Amesbury Archer and now talking to Mike made me see that period of prehistoric time for what it was: a well-connected and thriving European world with Britain and British metal reserves playing a fundamental role. Then there was Ireland. I said how I'd stood on the North Cornish coast the week before with John Fanshawe and stared out across the waters to where Ireland lay; how we had traced a rough route for the Bronze Age seafarers. Mike nodded.

'Well, we know about their boats as well, thanks to the Dover boat and others,' he agreed. 'It's a properly maritime society. So, of course, they're going to be in contact with Ireland and Europe.'

It was exciting. It really was. I clasped the coffee cup in my hands to get a better grip on all this. The reality of the Bronze Age was expanding before me. There was a growing truth to the notion of pairs and small groups of Beaker people travelling the pathways of land and sea, not just through Britain and Ireland, but across continental Europe. That scenario of me and Paul walking some ancient pathway across southern Britain as two Bronze Age beaker folk had some justification. They brought the emergent gold and copper metalworking skills that would lead to the Bronze Age but where had the rituals of mummification come from?

While I had the chance I wanted to ask more about those Cladh Hallan composite bodies. They still seemed utterly extraordinary to our modern eyes.

We started to talk mummies and specifically of that 'female' composite mummy with the torso of a woman, a male head and those incisors placed in each hand. Mike explained the scientific probability model: how there was a two-thirds likelihood the skull was at least seventy years older than the body. I started to think in generations again.

'So are they saying "This is grandfather's head"?' I asked.

'Well, I don't know,' said Mike. 'It could be. To misquote Lady Bracknell "One would be carelessness; two looks like it's deliberate"'.

I laughed.

'It certainly seems to be deliberate. It's not a matter of sending the stupid boy to the mummy shed and he comes back with the wrong bit...'

We both laughed.

'Because there was that kneecap that was found outside the roundhouses at Cladh Hallan,' I said. 'Red herring, you think?'

'No, not at all,' said Mike. 'What's important about it is that it shows there is breaking up of the bodies before they are actually posited in the ground. Why they take that kneecap and put it in that pit, I just don't know.'

'It's not practical?' I suggested.

'No. There's no practical sense in doing that,' said Mike. 'But for us it was a hugely important lead because it showed us they were breaking up these bodies long after death and yet they were still in articulation. It was a contradiction. It's the nature of the bone break. If you break old bone that's lost its collagen, it's like breaking a biscuit. But new bone you get a green fracture.'

'So you can tell from that.'

'Yes. You can tell from that. For it to be in articulation, as we found it, the skeleton had to have been held together by soft tissue and yet the bone was telling us it was very old.'

Even though it had been told many times before, as Mike retold the unveiling of the truth about those Cladh Hallan mummies, there was a tangible tension to the tale.

'That must have quite been a moment,' I said.

'Of course, we didn't realise until we were back in the lab.'

You could picture the scene: a gathering of the archaeologists in their lab coats and a dawning realisation enveloping them as to the dramatic truth they were uncovering. Yet those bodies hadn't given up all their secrets. Though Mike and his team had managed to collect enough DNA to tell that the head was from a separate individual from the body, and from that of the right leg, that ancient DNA sample wasn't sufficient to say whether those three individuals were related. But the science of DNA was improving.

'One day we will do that,' said Mike. 'It's on the back burner.'

One day. That was how our knowledge of prehistory evolved. One day someone discovered something else utterly remarkable that shifted accepted scientific thinking and then gradually that knowledge found its way out to the wider world. Chris Standish's analysis of prehistoric gold had been one such day. That moment in Mike's lab was another.

The revelation of the composite nature of that skeleton had caused a seismic, a paradigmatic, shift in the study of Bronze Age Britain. One day in the future, when there was funding and time, the individual bodies that made up those mummies of Cladh Hallan might be proved to be kith or kin. Perhaps some Bronze Age composite skeletons would be shown to be a kin construct – made from a family united across generations. And perhaps other skeletal figures will be shown to be built from the great and the good of the community – a society united in death.

As I walked out of the Institute of Archaeology and across Gordon Square, I was suddenly struck with a thought. It was to do with kneecaps. Mike had said how he was at a loss to explain the kneecap being taken from the female skeleton on South Uist and buried in a separate pit. And then I remembered that the Amesbury Archer was also missing a kneecap. Part of me wanted to head back to Mike's office. But he was busy enough without me bothering him. And anyway, I was due at the British Museum. I would just have to let the matter of the kneecaps go for the moment. They would have to sit with the teeth. I'd asked Mike about those incisors placed in each hand of the composite female skeleton – the left in the left hand, the right in the right. He confessed he had never seen it anywhere else.

There were still so many unknown pieces to the puzzle.

As I headed into the British Museum, I was still thinking of mummies. I stepped across the threshold and into the imperial grandeur of the entranceway. The wide, sweeping stone staircase on my left would lead me up to the rooms of ancient Egypt. I now knew that those mummies of Egypt laid out in the galleries above me had British counterparts. Britain, too, now officially had its own era of mummification.

Yet I hadn't come to see mummies. I had come to see Neil Wilkin, who was curator of the European Bronze Age collection. He met me in the wide-open space of the Great Hall. I could still remember when this universe had been the British Library and I had stepped about the desks beneath that beautiful, blue-globed roof seeking the seats where Sigmund Freud and Karl Marx had once sat. I had spent a good deal of my twenties in the various rooms of the British Museum. Based on his job title I had rather expected Neil to be some aged and estranged figure, lost to the ways of the past. He wasn't. He was young and engaging and he immediately elicited my utter delight by leading me through a labyrinth of hidden alleyways prohibited to the public. I was suddenly backstage in the British Museum.

We popped out of the maze at the staff canteen.

'Coffee or tea?' Neil asked.

I reckoned I'd need a coffee. I did. We sat and talked of ancient wonders. Neil handed me a colour image of the Ringlemere and the Rillaton Cup in all their golden glory. Side by side you could see their similarities. They really were twins.

'The Queen's got it,' I said pointing to the Rillaton Cup.

'Yes. It's in the Royal Collection,' said Neil. 'And we've got the Ringlemere Cup upstairs that was found by a metal detectorist.'

I had seen the cup when it had first arrived at the British Museum some years back. Neil pointed out the same pressed gold patterning in both – the same patterning used on the Mold Cape.

'So there's this tradition of embossing gold in this way,' explained Neil.

'And they all date from the same period?' I said.

'From around 2200 BC,' said Neil. 'Right through to about 1700 BC. The cape is at the end of that spectrum. And what we tend to think of is that these come earlier...'

Then he produced a photo of the museum's four sun discs. It was a lovely theatrical moment.

'So these and the lunulae found are very similar in that they're about cutting sheets of gold and then decorating them.'

'Right,' I said. 'And they're worn as some sort of solar symbolism?'

'Could well be,' agreed Neil.

He talked of the work of Mary Cahill whose ideas on sun discs and their mimicry of the various patterns of the sun on water I had so marvelled at.

'She's made a pretty convincing case over the years.'

He turned back to the picture of the sun discs.

'And what I particularly like is the way it's decorated with all the Beaker motifs.'

I had never really noticed that – a commonality in the patterning.

'So what you've got is Beaker pots and people coming from the continent at a time of enormous changes. Like metal. These people were discovering it. The Amesbury Archer captures it beautifully. So all these technologies are sweeping into Britain but they're not going into Ireland. So in Ireland, they don't practise the standard type of Beaker burial with the pots. They do their own thing. And one of the things they do, is to make these objects in gold ...'

Neil pointed back to the sun discs.

'But look,' he said and pointed to the cross-hatched pattern on one of the discs. 'A nod to the Beaker culture, to those ideas.'

He clearly loved the sun discs, too.

We talked over our coffees of that ratio of Irish to British sun discs and how more sun discs were now being found in Britain thanks to metal detecting, how the Irish finds that had largely come from cutting peat seemed to be drying up.

'But even though the numbers of sun discs in Britain might be going up,' said Neil. 'It's still the case that the best examples are from Ireland.'

Neil talked of how there was good evidence of copper travelling from its source at Ross Island in Ireland up into Scotland. Then we talked of gold – how the era known as the Copper Period or 'Chalcolithic' could just as easily be seen as the gold period, and how, so soon afterwards, there followed the beginnings of the Bronze Age.

'The Amesbury Archer has those very fine copper daggers and those gold ornaments,' said Neil. 'But no Bronze.'

I was juggling various dates in my head.

Neil put me straight. The Amesbury Archer was around 2300 BC. The Bronze Age was normally seen to start around 2200 BC.

'So one hundred years or so later you start to see tin and bronze...'

'Which is only four generations,' I said.

'Exactly.'

'That's nothing,'

Neil told of the dagger grave finds from Rameldry in Fife and the work of Neil Burridge from Cornwall who replicated those Early Bronze Age weapons. I mentioned Will Lord.

'Son of John Lord,' Neil said with due reverence.

He told of watching John Lord flint-knapping as a young student of archaeology some years back. Then he showed a jet necklace from the Rameldry site with clear similarities to the patterning on the sun discs. Then he told of a body of a man discovered there who dated from 2200 to 2000 BC.

'He was found with jet buttons from Whitby and one of them was inlaid with tin ...'

'Tin? I said. 'From Fife?'

'Inlaid with tin and found in Fife. And he has another button which was made of lizardite. They think the source of that is probably Cornwall.'

My head was spinning again. It wasn't merely the coffee. Neil's words had had their own effect. I was gazing back into a slim window of prehistoric time when the Beaker people were bringing new ways and technologies into Britain. There was the wonder of those golden sun discs and lunulae. Gold and copper working was soon to be followed by the forging of another metal form: Bronze. And after that, nothing would be the same again.

It had been another mesmerising day. I was ready to head home. And then Neil told me of something else from prehistory that was even more wondrous.

'It's called the Nebra Sky Disc,' he said.

He showed me a picture.

'It's a copper-alloy bronze disc with gold inlays. The gold is from Cornwall, though the disc was deposited near Halle in central Germany.'

We were huddled conspiratorially in a corner of the canteen. It felt I was being told a long-lost secret. Around us people chatted and drank their drinks. Cutlery clattered in the kitchen nearby.

I leaned closer to examine the colour photocopy. The disc was utterly stunning. It was composed of a blue, copper alloy face that had been inlayed with gold to represent the stars and the moon in various phases. I went silent.

'What it shows is the night sky and the sun and the crescent moon,' said Neil.

His excitement was evident. I was simply stunned.

'But it's been modified. It's had multiple lives. The theory is that it allows you to balance the solar and lunar calendars so you can know when to insert leap years in order to keep your calendars in sync.'

I was still gazing at the photocopy.

'Seven stars,' I said finally.

On the disc was a depiction of the seven stars of the Pleiades, the Seven Sisters.

The Nebra Sky Disc was far larger than any of the gold sun discs.

'It's dinner-plate size,' said Neil.

It also dated from later than the sun discs – probably around 1600 BC. And it was far more complex.

'It's an ancient astronomical instrument,' said Neil. 'If you buy into it ...'

Some moments later, I stumbled out of the British Museum rather dazed and confused. I had managed a few words of thanks and farewell to Neil Wilkin but now wandered on to the streets of Bloomsbury with my mind befuddled, full with musings on another ancient wondering.

My journeys into prehistory so far had taken me the length and breadth of Britain. I had dug ever deeper into the minds and beliefs of those souls who lived upon these lands thousands of years before us and it had become ever more evident that to understand ancient British ways and practices, you had to see these lands in relation to Europe. Eight thousand years ago, Doggerland had physically linked Britain to the continent. Then Britain had become separated. In the Neolithic Age, while there had certainly been a sense of cultural practices being shared across these islands, as the spread of stone circles and the development of agriculture illustrated, Britain had been more isolated then, more inward looking. By the Bronze Age, travel had extended beyond voyages around the islands of the British and Irish archipelago. People were now voyaging back and forth to continental Europe.

I thought of the Amesbury Archer, with his gold hair tresses and exquisite Beaker pottery, and his knowledge of the alchemic arts of metalworking, who had found his way from the heights of the Alps to his final resting place in the soils of Wiltshire. Metal trading had wrought such a significant shift to ancient ways of being. I heard Will Lord's line on how the Bronze Age was killing him as it echoed in my head. Then I heard Mike Parker Pearson's words from earlier that day: Bronze Age mummification like that discovered at Cladh Hallan was likely to be found across Europe. Bronze Age burial rites were apparently Pan-European. And then I thought again of the Nebra Sky Disc that had been unearthed in central Germany, but whose gold had come from Cornwall. I saw a map of prehistoric Britain and Europe before me with a series of black lines criss-crossing and steadily enmeshing the land, which signified the journeys made in distant times, the movements of highly skilled people, of gold and of tin, of the finest flint arrowheads, of Bronze axes and swords, of jet and of jewellery ... and of astronomical instruments.

I shook my head. I stopped. I stood while London whirled about me. Once more, I pictured the Nebra Sky Disc with its face of copper and gold, the pattern of the moon, the sun, the Pleiades. I had to see it in the flesh. I would follow the trail of that ancient Cornish gold to Halle in central Germany. I would venture over the seas, beyond the prehistoric worlds of Britain to those of mainland Europe. I glanced back to the stone façade of the British Museum, then turned and walked away.

ACKNOWLEDGEMENTS

IN MEMORY OF MICHAEL ALDERTON

I would like to thank the following people above all: my partner Katie Dawson, my sister Helen Canton and my mother Margaret Canton, my children Eva, Molly and Joe Canton, my uncle John Canton, Anthony Dee, Paul Gwynne, Peter Hulme, Juliet Lockhart, Sara Maitland, Ellie Mead, Jane Winch and my agent Jessica Woollard. Each has been an essential part in bringing *Ancient Wonderings* to life and I want to state here how extremely grateful I am to them for their various forms of support, guidance, advice and expertise.

As I set off on each individual wondering there were so many people that generously gave their guidance and help. Then there were others who offered wise words and thoughts from closer to home or helped me to secure the time and space needed to write the book. I wish to thank them all: Nick Ashton, Abdul Kareem Atteh, Ronald Blythe, Mary Cahill of the National Museum of Ireland, Mark Cocker, Bryony Coles, Ashley Cooper, Rosaline Cracknell, Jane and Desmond Crone, Phillip Crummy of Colchester Archaeological Trust, Howard Davis, Lola, Maureen and Peter Dawson, Tim Dennis, Professor David Dumville, John Fanshawe, Andrew Fitzpatrick, Susan Forsythe, Sally Foster, Godfrey and Lesley Goddard, Chris and Judy Gosling, Martin Gosling, Ros Green, Claire Halley, Doc Holliday, Jim Lock, Will Lord and his able assistant Simon, Kate MacDonald of Uist Archaeology, Rob Macfarlane, Adrian May, Chris McCully, Joe Newton, Mel Nice, Peter Nichols, Susan Oliver, Mike Parker Pearson, Emilia Pásztor, Colin Peel, Harry Perkins, Craig Perry, Aldous Rees, the staff of the Rare Books and Music Reading Room at the British Library, Jordan Savage, Molly Shrimpton, Chris Standish, Phil Terry, Beth Thomas, Owen Thompson and Jessica Trethowan of English Heritage, Louise Tunnard, Owain Hughes, and Anthony Hawley of Salisbury Museum, Anna Tyacke, Sara Chambers and Michael Harris of the Royal Museum of Cornwall, Ian Warrell, and Neil Wilkin of the British Museum.

To those at William Collins who have worked so hard on the book I also offer my thanks and especially so to Myles Archibald, Tom Cabot, Julia Koppitz, Katherine Patrick and Justine Taylor.

There are certainly others whose names I did not gather but met along the way whether in cities, towns, wildernesses, fields or byways. To all those anonymous souls who have also played a part in helping me on this long journey I send my thanks too.

INDEX

Note: the section dividers used throughout the text are constructed from the symbols for ancient tumuli of various sizes used on Ordnance Survey Maps in the 'Six-inch England and Wales, 1842–1952' series.